Mini Lessons for Revision

Mini Lessons for Revision

How to Teach Writing Skills, Language Usage, Grammar, and Mechanics in the Writing Process

Susan Geye

"That is question now;
And then comes answer like an Absey book.
King John, 4, 9
Shakespeare

ABSEY & CO.
SPRING, TX

DEDICATION

Some teachers possess the courage and determination to be pioneers of change in education, accepting the fact that change is necessary in order to meet the needs of today's students and striving to fulfill that need. Two such teachers, Becky Dickmann and Becky Tomlinson, and others like them stand strong against resistance and criticism from colleagues, as well as challenges from students and parents. Teachers like them have not only reevaluated and changed their teaching philosophy, but have successfully implemented and altered their way of teaching to fit that philosophy. Teachers like them teach with enthusiasm and energy, loving what they do and doing it better than excellent. Teachers like them make an impact on their students, changing their lives and attitudes.

Queries regarding rights and permissions should be addressed to:

Absey & Co.
23011 Northcrest
Spring, Texas 77389
281-257-2340

Published by Absey & Co., Spring, Texas.
Manufactured in the United States of America

ISBN 1-888842-04-0 (paper)

CONTENTS

ACKNOWLEDGMENTS

In February 1995 I mentioned to Joyce Armstrong Carroll and Edward E. Wilson, Directors of New Jersey Writing Project in Texas, that I had thirty or so minilessons I was thinking about compiling in a booklet to share with other teachers. They thought it was a great idea and mentioned it to the editor at Absey & Co. who wrote me a letter asking for my manuscript. I thought the letter was a form letter until Joyce called and asked me if I had heard from Absey & Co. They believed I could write this book and so did my fellow teachers and administrators.

Their constant encouragement and support motivated me to begin in earnest the writing of this book. I would like to acknowledge them and say, "Thank You, Thank You, Thank You! I owe you a debt of gratitude for helping make my dream come true."

Joyce Armstrong Carroll and Edward E. Wilson planted the seed of this dream in my mind and watered it until it bloomed.

Dr. Betty Carter, professor of Children and Young Adult Literature at Texas Woman's University, inspired me to step out of my comfort zone, then showed me how to make my dream a reality by guiding me through the writing and publication process.

Don Daniel, Assistant Superintendent at Crowley Independent School District, and LeeAnn Pyeatt, Administrative Assistant at Crowley Independent School District, provided the opportunity for me to learn how to teach writing, and their never failing confidence gave me the freedom and courage to take risks. Mr. Daniel loaned me his Macintosh Power Book on which to write this book; the convenience this afforded me saved valuable time and effort.

Becky Tomlinson, English teacher extraordinaire, proofread and edited my rough draft with skilled precision and an expert eye. Her suggestions made the lessons easier to follow, and the ideas she contributed to the lessons enhanced them.

Becky Dickmann, a truly gifted elementary teacher, read and reread the introduction, chapter overviews, and afterword, offering suggestions to make them clearer and more concise.

Kathryn Yockstick and Kay McCormack, excellent teachers from Crowley Independent School District, contributed valuable minilessons, making this book more beneficial to teachers.

Teachers at conferences, teachers on the internet, teachers' articles in magazines, and teachers down the hall shared ideas and suggestions that are within the pages of this book. When I knew who gave me an idea, I gave them credit, but most of the time I did not know.

Students diligently and patiently followed my instructions making suggestions that have improved the minilessons. Some of the examples and many of the ideas I used in this book have come from the writings my students have shared.

My children, Royce and Rexine, suggested ideas, words, and sentences for the examples included in these pages.

My husband, Tony, patiently loved me through the process of writing this book. His confidence in my ability kept me writing when I wanted to give up, and the emotional support he gave never failed to lift my spirits.

FOREWORD

Every year parents send their children to school for approximately 180 days, entrusting teachers with almost 1300 hours of each youngster's life. They give this time as an act of faith, expecting it to be used wisely for educating their children and helping them develop the tools for lifelong learning. As teachers, we accept this gift, knowing full well the responsibility it entails. That you respect such trust showed the moment you picked up this book. Why? You teach writing and you want to do it better.

Currently, the list of teaching "don'ts" would fill several blackboards: don't teach grammar in isolation, don't fit each assignment into a five paragraph box, and don't expect fine writing to develop solely through homework, to name a few. But, what are the deciding "do's"? Pat answers such as "teach the child at the point of need" or "teach through the child's own writing," come from a sound philosophical base but offer little guidance for turning that theory into practice. Without solid suggestions and classroom tested activities, teachers who want to teach the process of writing are like individuals who know they should lose weight but don't have any information on diet and exercise: they have good intentions for beginning a program, but lacking practical advice, quickly return to bad habits. As one beginning teacher said to me: "I understand the writing. It's the process that gets me."

The process is what this book is about. Here are activities to help children organize their thoughts, express them coherently, and edit them beyond a spelling check. You'll find model lesson plans covering such elements as paragraphing, determining audience, selecting a point of view, varying sentence patterns and length, eliminating sentence fragments, making subjects and verbs agree, punctuating dialog, and proofreading final drafts. In addition, there are suggestions for evaluation ranging from teacher evaluation to peer evaluation to self evaluation. These activities contain sound objectives, fit into the structure of a school day, use youngsters' own writings, and require no special materials. They come from the experience, the knowledge, and the practice of a fine teacher. Like parents who share their children's time, Susan Geye has given us a great gift: the gift of ideas. Accept it and use it well.

Betty Carter
Texas Woman's University

INTRODUCTION

Teaching writing challenges the best, most experienced teachers and often terrifies a beginning teacher. Standing in front of thirty disgruntled students scowling at the writing assignment is enough to make all teachers shake in their shoes and run for the nearest supply of aspirin. And, if the scowling faces don't do the trick, the thought of spending countless hours grading those one hundred-plus-papers, written on similar topics will definitely start the shakes, trembles, and headaches.

The purpose of this book is to show teachers that writing does not have to be a negative experience for them or their students but can actually be enjoyable and rewarding. Teaching students to write is more than assigning a topic or even allowing a student to choose a topic. And teaching writing as a process is more than prewriting, writing a rough draft, and finally recopying the rough draft for a final copy.

Textbooks are full of writing process "how to" explanations, but writing as a process is not a complete process unless teachers teach revision and editing skills. It is in these stages of the process that teaching writing skills, language usage, grammar, and mechanics have relevance. Using minilessons, a term popularized by Lucy Calkins, to teach these skills in the context of a student's writing will help students see the value in knowing how to write clear and concise prose. Students must be given the opportunity to apply these skills to their rough drafts before writing a final copy.

When teachers teach the skills students need to be writers and give students the freedom to make decisions and choices about their writing, students will be motivated to learn and apply the tools authors use in their craft, thereby becoming better writers.

Why Teach Minilessons?

The lessons in this book, based on brain research, are designed for optimal student learning. According to Dr. David A. Sousa, author of *How the Brain Learns*, new information needs to be conveyed to students in segments of twelve to fifteen minutes, and the optimum learning time is the first twelve to fifteen minutes of class when students are focused on the teacher. Minilessons allow the teacher to teach the skill within that time period, then in the time less optimal for conveying information, students complete the guided practice with other students and apply the skill they learned to their writing.

Also according to Dr. Sousa, in order for information to transfer from short to long term memory, it must be relevant to the learner. The information must make sense or have meaning; and, if both sense and meaning are present, the probability for permanent storage is even greater. Therefore, when students write about something important to them, it has meaning. Also, the immediate application of the writing skill to their own writing will make sense because these skills are necessary for writers to understand what they have written.

Minilessons also allow the student to practice the skill taught, and practice helps transfer the information from short to long term memory. The students practice the skill three times on the day it is taught: once with the teacher, once with other students, and once individually. Then, they practice the skill again when they proofread and with every piece they write throughout the year. This continual practice makes the skill a permanent part of their memory.

Working in cooperative groups helps the students gain confidence in their writing ability. Lev Vygotsky, a Russian cognitive developmentalist, believed that "What the child can do in cooperation today he can do alone tomorrow" (Vygotsky 104). The cooperative group techniques used in these minilessons allow the students to talk about what they are learning while applying it to their writing. This enables them to learn using visual, verbal, and auditory skills, once again increasing the probability of information being transferred to their long term memory while giving them confidence in their ability to write.

Teaching writing skills, grammar, and mechanics in the context of a student's writing forces the student to use the higher-order thinking skills developed by Benjamin Bloom—analysis, synthesis, and evaluation. When students apply these skills on a regular basis, they gain the ability to think abstractly. This results in improved critical thinking skills which benefits them in all subject areas.

Minilessons also give teachers the opportunity to individualize their curriculum, teaching students what they need. The knowledge and ability levels of students in one class vary greatly. When students relate skills to their own writing, they gain a better understanding of how to apply those skills on their level. Individualizing the curriculum creates an authentic learning opportunity, thus facilitating transfer of information relevant to the learner from short to long term memory.

How to Teach Minilessons

The minilessons in this book are written to be teacher friendly by providing a stated objective, a list of materials needed by the teacher and student, easy-to-follow directions, and sufficient examples to illustrate rules and guidelines. Developing a method for keeping track of individual student progress is a crucial factor in making the lessons successful. Constantly circulating the room to answer students' questions will keep the teacher abreast of student progress and will motivate the students to stay on task.

What to Teach and When to Teach It?

The minilessons in this book are applicable to all writing in all modes for all purposes with the possible exceptions of the three narrative lessons:
- "Creating Characters with Life"
- "Using Dialog Appropriately,"
- "Punctuating Dialog"

Determining which lessons to teach first depends largely on the needs of the students and requirements of the scope and sequence; however, I almost always teach the following on the first writing assignment:
- "Hooking the Reader with a Dynamite Lead"
- "Making the Middle Clear and Concise"
- "Show, Don't Tell Using Imagery"
- "Using Pronouns and Antecedents Correctly"
- "Using *be* Verbs Sparingly"
- "Comma Rules Made Easy"

I teach these lessons first because they form a strong base upon which to build more specific tools, and I want to hold students accountable for the above six lessons on every writing assignment they complete all year long. I determine which lessons to teach next based on the needs of the students ascertained after grading their first papers. They vary from year to year.

To those teachers apprehensive about covering the required skills on the scope and sequence, rest assured even more will be covered. To justify this, keep a list of the skills taught, and when they were taught, including the skills presented within a particular minilesson. For example, all of the grammar concepts covered in the minilesson "Combining Sentences" should be listed, and listed again when many of those same skills are taught in "Varying Sentence Beginnings" and "Varying Sentence Patterns and Lengths." Teaching the same skill several times with different applications enables the students to gain a broader base of knowledge for manipulating language and gives them ample opportunity to practice the application of the skill.

Additionally, minilessons are a springboard for teachable moments, such as exceptions to the rules arising when students revise their own papers. This affords the teacher opportunities to teach higher levels of grammar and sentence structure. Skills taught during teachable moments are skills that should be noted on the list of skills kept.

Materials the Teacher Needs

Included in each lesson are all the necessary examples, sample passages, definitions, or how-to explanations. These items are located at the end of each lesson, and the type is larger so it can be seen easier on an overhead projector. These pages can be enlarged on a poster machine, copied to hand out to students, or copied on a transparency. The materials are listed at the beginning of each lesson, but the following list contains all of the materials needed:

tape	correction fluid
3 x 5 cards	5 x 7 cards
scissors	butcher paper
construction paper	colored markers
transparencies	paper clips
dictionaries	thesauri
sentence strips	sticky notes
sticky tack for walls	grammar books
different colors of transparency pens	

Materials the Students Need

Students will need a rough draft before they can apply the skills taught in the minilessons. Most of the time, I teach minilessons when my students are working on a major writing assignment. However, since I do not teach more than six lessons per paper, occasionally I teach a grammar minilesson and have students apply the skill to prewriting from a journal entry or other prewriting activities. Evidence of this skill is expected on their next assignment.

Students also need a spiral notebook for taking notes. They are required to take notes on every skill taught so they will have a personalized grammar handbook. The first five pages are reserved for a table of contents, and students number the remaining pages. This helps them locate the notes they need when they need them.

Helpful Tips

• The lessons in this book are planned for use within a fifty-five minute period but can easily be adapted to shorter or longer blocks of time.

• Only run copies of a handout for every student if the handout will be used for guided practice. It has been my experience that copies of notes end up on the floor or lost; therefore, I copy a class set of the handout and instruct the students to write the notes in their spiral notebook.

• Instruct students to write their rough drafts on one side of the paper only, skipping every other line, and in one color of ink. This practice makes the revision process much easier for them. They can add information between the lines, cut their paper apart to move a para

graph, then tape it back together, and make their revisions in a different color of ink so they will know what they have changed.

• Check students' revisions frequently during the revising process so that it is not necessary to pick up the rough drafts with the final copy. This cuts down on the paper load.

• Daily grades can be given for class participation, group activities, and correct application of the skills taught.

• Occasionally, require students to turn something in at the end of the period—a list, a grid, or a revision. This helps keep them on task and holds them accountable.

• Use students who finish their revisions quickly to help students needing additional explanation or more guided practice. This gives students confidence in their ability to write.

• Celebrate student improvement by recognizing successful application of skills learned through minilessons presented.

• After teaching the minilessons in this book, you will be comfortable taking skills your students need and adapting them to fit the format.

Chapter 1

ORGANIZATION MAKES WRITING READABLE

Overview and Rationale

The minilessons in this chapter will show students how to:
- revise their rough drafts for logical organization
- focus the content of their rough drafts
- capture and maintain reader interest.

It is important to start teaching revision with broad concepts that affect the overall shape of the final piece. When students begin revision with organized rough drafts and with the content of their rough drafts focused, it is easier for them to revise words and sentences for style, grammar, and mechanics.

Minilesson 1

Skill
Hooking the Reader with Dynamite Leads

Objective
Students will be able to recognize quality leads, then reenter their rough draft to revise their lead for greater reader interest.

Materials
Teacher: class set of "Revising Your Lead"
             blank transparencies
Student: rough draft
             pen/pencil
             paper
             novel

Procedure
1. Explain:
"A good lead must hook the reader's attention and arouse their curiosity by being entertaining and/or interesting so the reader will continue reading. It should drop the reader into the middle of the action."

2. Ask several students to read the first paragraphs of their novels to the class. Comment on each lead and ask the students what they notice. Write their responses on the board.

3. Hand out "Revising Your Lead." Read and discuss it with the students and ask:
"Which techniques, if any, did the authors use in the leads we just read in class?"
New techniques may be discovered.

Application
1. Explain:
"Many times when you start to write a rough draft, you write unnecessary information or information that can be conveyed in the body through the use of dialog. It is often necessary for you to do this to begin writing. For example, if the topic is about when you were ten years old and fell in the pool with your clothes on, start the story with 'Splash!', then work the details into the story about how old you were, where you lived, the occasion, and what you wore. Begin the story where the story starts."

2. Instruct students to read their rough draft, looking for the true beginning. Explain:
"Some of you started at the beginning of your story, but many of you need to find the beginning. Read your rough draft and try to determine where your story actually begins. Which technique or techniques did you use from 'Revising Your Lead'?"

3. On a separate sheet of paper, instruct the students to choose two different techniques, then rewrite their lead twice, using each technique once, and stating the techniques used.

4. Divide students into groups of three. Each student should read all three leads to his or her group, then with group input, determine which lead is most effective for the intended audience and purpose.

Assessment
1. Ask every student to read their chosen lead. After the lead is read, ask the class to respond to its effectiveness for hooking the reader.

2. Ask several students to write their three leads on a transparency to use for models in class.

3. For a grade, pick up the three leads written and evaluate them for completion, technique, and interest.

Adapted from *In The Middle*

Minilesson 1

Transparency

REVISING YOUR LEAD

1. <u>Describe a character</u>:

Of the many explorers who have sought traces of Atlantis, none was more intrepid than Colonel Percy Harris Fawcett. A self-proclaimed lone wolf, he resolved to accomplish what no man before him had.

–Chris Huff

2. <u>Action</u>:

The ball whistled through the air toward the plate. I swung late, and the ball rocketed down the first line just out of reach of the diving first baseman.

–Brian Pearce

3. <u>Dialog</u>:

"Come down off the ledge, son!" yelled the police officer. "Your problems can be solved. Don't take your life."
Brad screamed at the officer, "You don't know me or my problems!"

–David Marsden

4. <u>Emotion</u>:

She could no longer endure the pain. Her tears subsided, but the sobs continued to wrack her body.

5. <u>Detail</u>:

Old man Higgins stopped his beat up Chevy on the side of the dirt road to watch the bright, disc-shaped light zig-zag across the night sky.

–Jon Gwodz

6. <u>Setting</u>:

My eyes dart nervously around the still, silent courtroom. The witness stand is empty, no jurors fill the box, and the judge's gavel lies inert on his desk.

7. <u>Quotation</u>:

"Live and let live," my old man used to say. He should have followed his own advice.

8. **Avoid leads that begin with**:

a rhetorical question:

What do you do with a million dollars?

phrases like:

When I was six...
or
I'll never forget the time...
or
One day...
or
I am going to tell you about...

Minilessons for Revision–©1997 Absey & Co., 23011 Northcrest, Spring, Texas 77389, 281.257.2340

Minilesson 2

Skill
Making the Middle Clear and Concise

Objective
Students will be able to examine the body of their rough drafts (narrative or essay) for clarity and cohesiveness, then reenter their rough drafts to make needed revisions.

Materials
Teacher: transparency of "Sample Passage to Model Revision"
Student: rough draft
pen/pencil
notebook paper

Procedure
1. Ask students:
"What kind of things are written in the middle of a piece of discourse? What is the purpose of the middle?"
Write their responses on the board.
2. If needed, supplement the students' responses by explaining:
"Once the writer hooks the readers' attention with the lead, the writer should strive to keep their attention. The middle should:
   - be clearly related to the lead,
   - be focused on the problem in the story or thesis of the paper
   - maintain momentum by continuing to advance and change
   - build toward the end while informing the readers of specific details or a sequence of events or developing ideas that were presented in the lead.
3. Ask students to write the audience and the purpose of their rough draft at the top of their paper because everything in the middle should relate to both. Refer to the first two questions in step 4. (For a more detailed lesson refer to "Determine Audience and Purpose" in Chapter 1.)
4. Tell students:
"When revising the middle of your paper, look for ways to make the writing more focused, more concentrated on content."
The following list of questions will help achieve focus. Write them on the board and have students copy them on a sheet of paper, leaving four or more lines between each question.

- Who is the audience for my paper? ex: friend? parents?
- Why am I writing this piece? State my purpose.
  ex: to entertain, share personal experience
- What information is included that does not relate to my topic and audience?
- What questions have I left unanswered for the readers?
- How does the middle clearly relate to the lead?
- Where does the writing become dull and boring?
- Where do I need to add examples, details, illustrations, or anecdotes to clarify ideas or make a point?

5. When the students have finished copying the questions, put the "Sample Passage to Model Revision" on the overhead and model how to answer the questions with them, then revise the passage.

NOTE: This is a good opportunity for students to see the value in writing their rough draft on one side of the paper only, skipping every other line, and writing in one color of ink. Now, they can cut apart their draft and tape it together like they want it; they have room to add detail in between the lines or on the back, and a different color of ink will tell them what they have changed.

Possible Answers to the Questions
- Audience: peers
- Purpose: to entertain
- Leave out:
  Shelly remembers a movie...
  ...especially one little boy. He is crying...
  He tries to calm the passengers down...
  The flight attendants search for...
- Some unanswered questions:
  What went wrong with the plane?
  Was there a bomb?
  Does Shelly have a family?
  Wouldn't she think about loved ones if she thought she was going to die?
  Did the plane slide through the field

when it hit the ground?

What was going on after the crash besides screaming?

Were people killed?

- Related to lead:

Shelly's apprehension about flying was for a reason.

The middle tells why Shelly's eyes snap open.

- Dull and boring:

The piece isn't long enough to get dull and boring.

No long descriptions, useless dialog, or passages without action; these are the types of writing that get dull and boring.

- Write answers for the unanswered questions.

Application

1. Divide students into groups of three and instruct each student to read his or her rough draft to the group twice, the first time to listen and the second time to analyze. Listeners need to pay close attention to the reader so they can be prepared to address the questions written on the board. When students give the reader feedback, it needs to be written on the author's list of questions so the author will have it to use for revision.

2. Students work individually, making revisions while the teacher circulates to offer help and keep students on task.

3. When students have made the necessary revisions, allow them to return to their original group. They each read their revised rough draft to the group. The listeners comment on the effectiveness of the revisions and/or make new suggestions.

Assessment

1. Ask students to answer the following questions and add them to the list they had written earlier:

"Does your rough draft flow better?

Can you see the benefit of your revisions? Why?

How did your rough draft change?"

2. For a daily grade, pick up the list of questions at the end of class to evaluate the students on this procedure, then return it to them the next day so they can continue to make their revisions. Either way, this list should be turned in with the final copy.

Minilesson 2

Transparency

SAMPLE PASSAGE TO MODEL REVISION
BLOWN AWAY

Shelly's eyes close, and her muscles begin to relax when she realizes the plane made it safely in the air. Leaning her head back, she sinks into the cushioned pillow and slowly drifts to sleep. Suddenly, her eyes snap open.

The plane is jerking violently, and the captain announces that he has to make an emergency landing. Shelly remembers a movie she saw about a plane crash, but she couldn't remember how it ended. The flight attendants help everyone with their oxygen masks and tell people sitting by the emergency exits what to do when the plane is on the ground. The passengers panic, some quietly crying, others screaming, especially one little boy. He is yelling for his teddy bear which is in the overhead compartment.

The captain announces he will try to land the plane in an empty field. He tries to calm the passengers down by telling them he is a veteran pilot and knows what to do. The plane is falling faster toward the ground, and Shelly doesn't think the captain will be able to make a safe landing. Fear grips her heart and tears flood her eyes.

Moments after the announcement, the plane hits the ground. The sound of crushing metal and piercing screams fill the air. The smell of smoke is unbearable from the fire raging in the back of the plane, so the flight attendants search for fire extinguishers. Shelly tries to get to one of the emergency exits.

Stumbling over unconscious bodies and luggage that had fallen out of the overhead compartments, Shelly moves aimlessly through the smoky blackness. Suddenly, she feels intense heat and sees fire burning red. The force of the explosion sends her flying to her death.

Based on a story written by Marcy Miller

Minilesson 3

Skill
Concluding with a Bang

Objective
Students will be able to recognize when to conclude their narrative or essay, see how to write a satisfying conclusion, then reenter their rough drafts to revise their conclusions.

Materials
Teacher: transparency of "Revising Your Conclusion"

transparency of "Example Leads and Conclusions"

a class set of "Revising Your Conclusion"

blank transparencies

Student: rough draft

pen/pencil

paper

novel

Procedure
1. Explain:

"The conclusion of a piece should bring the story or essay to a satisfactory close for the reader. Think of the rough draft as separate parts connected by a string; the conclusion is the knot holding the parts together. Without a strong knot, the story falls apart. For this reason, the writer should put as much thought into the conclusion as into the lead."

2. Put the transparency of "Revising Your Conclusion" on the overhead. Ask students:

"Which of these techniques, if any, did the authors use on the conclusions just read?"

New techniques may be discovered.

3. Ask several students to read the first and last paragraphs of a novel, short story, or article. Comment on each reading based upon discussion of step 2 and ask the students what they notice. Write their responses on the board.

Application
1. Explain:

"One of the most difficult things about writing a conclusion is knowing when to stop. You stop when you have presented all of the important facts and ideas, and when you have made the points you want to make. Don't ramble on, boring the reader with unimportant details."

2. Read the rough draft, looking for the place the story ends, and stop.

3. When writing a conclusion, reread the introduction. Sometimes an effective conclusion will tie the two together, bringing the reader full circle or creating a frame.

4. Put the transparency of "Example Leads and Conclusions" on the transparency, then read and discuss with the class. Try to elicit from the students how the leads relate to the conclusion, how the two tie together.

5. Hand out "Revising Your Conclusion" and ask the students to determine which, if any, of the techniques they used in their conclusion.

6. Then, instruct students to choose two techniques they want to try that will fit their audience and purpose. Write the two different conclusions on a separate sheet of paper.

7. Divide students into groups of three, and instruct them to read their three conclusions, the original and two revised versions. With group input, students choose the most effective conclusion.

Assessment
1. Ask students to read the lead and the conclusion they chose. Ask the class to comment on effectiveness.

2. Ask several students to write their lead and two conclusions on a transparency to use as models for class.

3. Instruct students to turn in their lead and conclusion. This will help determine which students, if any, need additional help.

Minilesson 3

Transparency/Handout

REVISING YOUR CONCLUSION

1. **A Lesson Learned:**

> Finally, I could see the glass half full instead of half empty.

2. **Action**:

> As the football spiraled through the air, Jason ran down the field to be in a position to catch it. The ball landed right in his hands, and he ran it in for the winning touchdown.

3. **Dialog:**

> "Danny, I told you that I would be here for you, no matter what happened, and I meant it. Do you believe me now?"
>
> "I sure do! Thanks for sticking by me."

4. **Emotion**:

> As my parents leave the room, I lean back against the soft, comfortable couch and let the feelings of despair and loneliness envelop me.

5. **Drawstring**:

> Chris and I had been through a tough time together, but the trial had strengthened the bond between us. Never again would we doubt each other, and from that day on, we remained best friends.

6. **Surprise**:

> I ran home to see how I could help. I saw my family standing in the doorway with smiles on their faces. "GOTCHA!" they yelled. I had forgotten it was April Fool's Day, and it looked like I was the Fool.

7. **Quotation:**

> I can't even think about what I had done to deserve the pain I must now endure. I should have listened when Shelly told me, "What goes around, comes around."

Minilessons for Revision–©1997 Absey & Co., 23011 Northcrest, Spring, Texas 77389, 281.257.2340

Minilesson 3

Transparency

EXAMPLE LEADS AND CONCLUSION

1. A Lesson Learned

Lead:

Getting a driver's license is a rite of passage every teenager in America looks forward to, and I was no exception.

Conclusion:

When you see a young girl on the road, I advise you to pull over and let her have the rite of passage.

2. Creating a Frame

Lead:

Every Halloween Jason Scott sits in his rocking chair, waiting for the doorbell to ring. He brings out a bucket of candy and puts a handful in each child's bucket.

Conclusion:

I'll bet this next Halloween, Jason Scott will be handing out candy in heaven.

–Justen Murdock

3. Action

Lead:

I slid hard into first base, and held my breath, waiting for the umpire to make his call. "He's out!"

Conclusion:

The throbbing pain in my leg was almost too much to bear. A few guys from the other team picked me up and carried me to Dad's car. After my dad got in and shut his door, I cried, "I am safe ."

–Brian Pearce

4. Drawstring

Lead:

Jerry grasped the cold rock in his gloved hand, and carefully raised his foot to a small rock ledge. He tried to grasp another rock, but his numb fingers refused.

Conclusion:

The mountain, a taunting peak, had been conquered. Jerry had scaled the mountain using his physical skill, mental toughness, and unerring determination. He had won the battle.

Minilesson 4

Skill
Writing Effective Paragraphs

Objective
The students will be able to recognize the reasons for paragraphing, then revise their rough drafts for effective paragraphs.

Materials
Teacher: 4 different colors of transparency pens
copies of "Sample Passage without Paragraphs" for every student
8 to 10 magazines
2 cans of soda, 1 grape and 1 orange
Student: rough draft
pen/pencil
novel

Procedure
1. One theory addressing the evolution of paragraphing has its roots in medieval times. Monks would draw elaborate pictures around the first letter of the first word on the page in order to provide a visual break from the text. The book *Illuminations* by Jonathon Hunt offers an example of illumination.

2. Ask students:
"Are paragraphs necessary? Why do writers use paragraphs?" Write their responses on the board. Some responses are listed below, but students should think of more.
    change in the action
    keep the reader's interest
    make transitions
    develop an idea
    change of setting
    emphasize a point
    changes in time
    dialog

3. In order to demonstrate the idea of making new paragraphs, show students a can of orange soda and a can of grape soda. Tell them orange soda is all they will ever find in an orange soda can, and grape soda is all they will ever find in a grape soda can. This concept is also true in writing; similar ideas are contained in one paragraph. To illustrate indention, make a dent in the can. It now has an indent. So, all similar ideas or dialog spoken by a character, needs to be in one paragraph (container) with an indention.

4. Hand out the magazines to students and ask the remaining students to look in their novels to find paragraphs that serve as examples of the reasons they brainstormed. Students should state the reason, then read the paragraph. Other students may agree or disagree.

5. Explain:
"Paragraphs are a writer's building blocks made up of well developed sentences with varied patterns, giving meaning and organization to writing."

Students should write this definition and the list of reasons in their notebooks.

6. Hand out "Sample Passage without Paragraphs" and instruct students to place the ¶ symbol where they think a paragraph should begin.

7. When students have completed the handout, ask one student where he or she placed the paragraphs and the reasons why. Mark them in one color on the transparency, writing the reason in the margin closest to the ¶ symbol. Then, ask another student the same questions, marking the ¶ in a different color. Repeat this step with three or four students. Then ask:
"Did anyone place a paragraph anywhere that is not marked?"

If so, mark it on the transparency.

8. Point out that although the reasons for making a paragraph were on the board, the paragraphs were placed differently by different students. Ask students:
"Why?" They should be able to verbalize that they interpreted the meaning differently."

Refer them to the definition for clarification.

Application
1. Explain to students a few paragraph guidelines:
• When writing dialog, a new paragraph should begin every time the speaker changes.
• To keep the reader's interest, avoid overly long paragraphs. It is better to make two or three short paragraphs.

2. Ask students to look at the pages in their novels or in a magazine article to see the length of paragraphs authors use. Also, ask students about what they prefer when they read—short or long paragraphs? Relating their reading to their writing will help them see their writing as

a reader would.

3. Instruct students to read their rough drafts as if there were no paragraphs, inserting the ¶ symbol where a paragraph should begin based on the meaning they want to convey and the list on the board. Some students will already have paragraphs and may just want to write our their reasons for paragraphing. Students should write the reason for each paragraph in the margin by the symbol.

4. Suggest to students they may need to move a sentence to a different place in the paragraph or the rough draft. They might find a sentence that needs to be omitted because the information is not necessary or is unrelated to the topic. (see "Making the Middle Clear and Concise") They may also need to add a transition. (see "Transitions Make Writing Coherent") Instruct students to make these revisions.

Assessment

Instruct students to exchange their rough drafts with a partner, then read each other's paper for paragraph placement. If there are any questions about the paragraph placement or any additional suggestions for changes that could be made, students should discuss them with each other .

Minilesson 4

Transparency/Handout

SAMPLE PASSAGE WITHOUT PARAGRAPHS

The College Football Hall of Fame, located in downtown South Bend, Indiana, combines historic memorabilia with state-of-the-art interactive exhibits. This hands-on, sports museum is the largest of its kind. The parking lot is painted to look like a football field, complete with grid lines and goal posts, and pennantes from the top twenty-five ranking college teams hang from a team helmet in the foyer. A forty-three foot sculpture depicts the life of a football player from childhood to manhood, and from there, the history of college football unfolds in unique and entertaining ways. Window displays exhibit the evolution of the football, the football field, the football stadium, and the players' uniforms and equipment. The stadium theater has ten movie screens surrounding the room showing film clips of famous college football plays, coaches giving half-time pep talks, football players, marching bands, cheerleaders; and sports fans fill every screen and change every thirty seconds. Surround sound adds reality to the experience. Also, ten interactive CD-ROM players throughout the museum allow visitors to look up information about college players, coaches, and team statistics by touching a designated spot on the screen. Visitors can test their passing, kicking, and running skills on a practice field, and machines in the fitness room measure agility, strength and endurance. The College Football Hall of Fame is a monument to college football and the players and coaches who made it great. Football fans owe a debt of gratitude to The National Football Foundation, who bring together all of the organized groups involved in amateur football, for their effort in making a walk through college football history possible.

Minilessons for Revision–©1997 Absey & Co., 23011 Northcrest, Spring, Texas 77389, 281.257.2340

Minilesson 5

Skill
Transitions Make Writing Coherent

Objective
Students will be able to identify transitions and recognize the need for them in writing, then reenter their rough drafts to add transitions at appropriate places.

Materials
Teacher: transparency of "Sample Passage with Transitions"
class set of "Transitions and Their Functions"
transparencies
transparency pens
Student: rough draft
pen/pencil
highlighter

Procedure
1. Ask students for a definition or example of the word *transition* and write their responses on the board. Although the definitions will vary, all can apply to writing. When students understand the word in other contexts, it will be easier for them to grasp the importance of using transitions in their writing.

2. Explain:
"In good writing, ideas are presented and connected in a clear, logical manner. Transitions used appropriately make writing coherent and clarify connections for reader."

3. Put "Sample Passage with Transitions" on the overhead and read it with the students. Ask them to identify the transitional words, phrases, and/or sentences and explain their purpose or function. Write their responses on the board which should include:

Thirty minutes later	to show time
Before we left	to show time
As soon as we	to show cause or reason
As we neared	to show location
Finally	to show time
Immediately	to show time
At Bobby's funeral	to show location

Point out other functions for which transitions can serve:
to introduce examples
to add more information
to contrast different ideas or objects
to conclude
to compare similar ideas or objects

4. Brainstorm other transition words or phrases students know, then write them under the above categories.

5. Ask students to read through their rough drafts, highlighting transition words, phrases, or sentences they have used. Ask several students who finish quickly to write their passage on a transparency, leaving out the transitions.

6. When all students have completed highlighting their rough drafts, put the student samples on the overhead and read them with the class. Ask:
"Does the writing flow smoothly without the transitions? Why not? Is the writing coherent without the transitions? Why not?"

7. Write the transitions in the samples and read it again. Students will hear the difference.

Application
1. Divide students into groups of three.

2. Instruct the students to read their rough drafts to the group. The listeners need to listen for incoherent passages, then tell the reader where transitions might be added. The author highlights the passages pointed out.

3. Hand out "Transitions and Their Functions" to each student. If needed, instruct them to add the words they brainstormed on the board that are not on the handout.

4. After student have read their rough drafts and received feedback from the group, the students need to work individually, adding the needed transitions to their rough drafts. Explain:
"First, determine the function of the transition, then choose the most appropriate transition word or phrase from the list."

Assessment
1. After students have had the opportunity to make revisions, the students regroup and reread their rough drafts. The students should be instructed to listen for how the transitions affected the flow and coherence of the writing and tell the author if the transition revisions were effective.

2. Ask one student from each group to share a before and after passage. Write several of them on a transparency to use as models for class.

Minilesson 5

Transparency

SAMPLE PASSAGE WITH TRANSITIONS
CRIP KILLERS

I was chillin' with my boy Crazy C at the mall, playing games in the arcade, talking to girls, and having fun. We called some homeys to pick us up, and thirty minutes later they arrived to take us home.

When we got home, we ate, then Crazy got beeped. He looked at his pager, and said, "I have to use the phone. Come on."

We walked to the phone, and Crazy called Bobby. He set up a meeting for thirty minutes later. Before we left, Crazy picked up his gun. That made me nervous, but I went anyway.

As soon as we stepped on the bus, we headed to Southside. As we neared our destination, I understood why Crazy C needed his gun. Graffiti covered the walls of buildings warning outsiders, set trippers, and slippers of their death. Crazy C and I wore blue, and all I could see was red. My heart pounded in my chest, and my hands were sweating. I knew we were headed for trouble.

Finally, we stepped off the bus and walked to JJ's to meet Bobby. We met him in the street, and just as we turned to walk in the joint, some punks drove by shooting. I heard gunshots, bullets screaming, and shells falling to the ground. Immediately, Crazy reached for his gun, but he took a bullet in his arm and fell. I ducked to avoid being hit, and Bobby lay on the sidewalk in a pool of blood. The shooting stopped almost as soon as it had started, but the suffering it caused would never be over.

At Bobby's funeral, his brothers placed a bullet under his jacket, then laid a blue rag on his chest. His death wouldn't stop the pointless and continuous cycle of violence.

Based on a story by Kenji Richardson

Minilesson 5

Transparency/Handout/Poster

TRANSITIONS AND THEIR FUNCTIONS

The following list is not inclusive; some of the more commonly used transitions were omitted due to space and familiarity.

Transitions Used to Introduce Examples:
    for example   for instance

Transitions Used to Show Time:

third	soon	later
first	meanwhile	before
earlier	second	subsequently
last	eventually	next

Transitions Used to Add Information:

also	in addition	furthermore	too

Transitions used to show location:

above	beyond	under
near	to the left/right	beneath
on top of	alongside	

Transitions Used to Contrast Different Ideas or Objects:

however	otherwise	although
even though	still	nevertheless
regardless	on the other hand	on the contrary

Transitions Used to Compare Ideas or Objects:

likewise	in the same way	similarly

Transitions Used to Conclude or Summarize:

as a result	therefore	all in all
in any event	without a doubt	after all

Transitions Used to Show Cause or Reason:

therefore	consequently	because
since	as a result	for this reason

Chapter 2

FINE TUNE THE FOCUS

Overview and Rationale

Writing that lacks focus and purpose is virtually impossible to understand. The students' writing meanders through a maze of confusion, never quite making the point intended — probably because the students did not know what point they intended to make or what idea they wanted to convey when they started writing. This is a common problem among student writers.

The minilessons in this chapter teach students how to fine tune the focus and purpose of their pieces, thereby eliminating confusion in their writing.

Minilesson 6

Skill
Determine Audience and Purpose

Objective
Students will be able to recognize the importance of audience and purpose, then reenter their papers to determine the most appropriate audience and purpose for their piece.

Materials
Teacher: butcher paper
          3 x 5 cards
          black markers
Student: rough draft
          pen/pencil
          paper

Procedure
1. Explain to students:

"Knowing who will be reading your writing (audience) will help you determine how you write, what details and examples to include, where to place emphasis, what level of vocabulary to use, which voice to use, and what tone to convey. Knowing why you are writing (purpose), will help you determine what to write. What is the point of your story, and how you will make it? When readers read your writing, will they respond with, *So what?* or will they know the reason behind or the point of your writing. Determining audience and purpose gives your writing focus, thereby making it easier to write."

2. Divide students in groups of three and give each group a card with a specific audience and purpose written on it, a black marker, and a 3 foot piece of butcher paper. Each group writes on the butcher paper about the school cafeteria for the audience and purpose written on the card. The groups need to keep their assignments to themselves. Listed are examples.

AUDIENCE
      PURPOSE
Eighth grade class
      Share a lesson learned.
          ex: get in line early, lines are long
Foreign exchange student
      Inform
          ex: cost of food
Principal
      Persuade to change something
          ex: put cokes in machines
Second grade class
      Describe
          ex: snack line
Parent
      Entertain with a funny story
          ex: food fight
Friend at another school
      Share emotional experience
          ex: slipped and fell
Friend from previous school
      Compare/Contrast
          ex: taste of food

3. When students have completed their writing, ask each group to read it to the class and post it on the wall. The writers will be able to judge their success if the students in the class can determine the correct audience and purpose for whom the writing was intended.

4. As groups read, ask the students to listen for and take notice of the differences between the writing. Then as they discuss the differences, write them on the board. Refer to *Procedure*, step 1 for a list of differences.

Application
1. Write the following questions on the board, then ask students to read their rough drafts to determine the answers:
      For whom am I writing?
          (audience)
      What point do I want to make?
          (purpose)
      What idea am I trying to convey?
          (purpose)
These will be difficult questions for some students to answer, but encourage them to persevere because without a specific audience and purpose their papers will lack focus.

2. Instruct students to write the questions and the answers and their working title on a separate sheet of paper to be turned in at the end of class.

Assessment
1. Before students leave the classroom, ask them to turn in the sheet of paper on which they have written their working titles and their questions and answers.

2. A daily grade could be taken for class participation and completion of the task.

Minilesson 7

Skill
Point of View Makes a Difference

Objective
Students will be able to recognize the strengths and weaknesses of differing points of view, then reenter their rough drafts to determine which points of view would be the most effective.

Materials
Teacher: transparency of "Sample Passages-First and Third Person Points of View"
Student: rough draft
pen/pencil
paper

Procedure
1. Put "Sample Passages-First and Third Person Points of View" on the overhead. After reading them, ask students what the difference is between the passages. They should be able to figure out the difference in point of view by the pronouns used.

2. Ask them:
"Why would one point of view be more effective than another? What are their individual strengths and weaknesses?"

Discuss their responses while writing them on the board.

3. Be sure the following ideas are covered. Point of view is the position from which the author observes his or her subject.

First Person: The most limited because the author is in the head of one character and can't come out. First person states, "I was there." The author becomes a participant in the story, and the strength is the intimacy between the writer and the reader.

Third Person: The most versatile because the author is an observer of the story and can be in the mind of one or more characters. The pronouns *he, she,* and *they* are used.

Application
1. To help students determine which point of view would be best for their paper, ask them to reread their rough drafts and answer the following questions:
• What point of view did you use in your rough draft? (first or third)
• How do you know? (pronouns used,

author is or is not a participant)
• Who tells the story? (which character or observer)
• Why? (because the story primarily happens to one character)

2. Other factors to consider are audience and purpose. Which point of view would further the purpose and be most effective for the intended audience? Discuss the possibilities with the students.

3. Before students make a decision, instruct them to rewrite the first paragraph in a different point of view on a separate sheet of paper. Of the two paragraphs, one in first person the other in third person, which do they think is most effective for the audience, purpose, and story?

Assessment
1. Divide students in small groups and ask them to read their two paragraphs to the group. The group can help the author determine which point of view is most effective.

2. Collect the two paragraphs and evaluate them based on completion and the correct use of the first and third points of view.

Minilesson 7
Transparency

SAMPLE PASSAGE
THIRD PERSON POINT OF VIEW

Steve's senior year had been awesome. He was dating the best looking girl in his class, his grades were above average, and he was going to be a starter on the basketball team. "Life couldn't be better," he thought as he walked to the gym.

Twenty guys stood in front of the bulletin board, anxiously scanning the cut list for their names. Shouts of joy and sighs of pain filled the hall as the guys learned whether or not they made the cut for the basketball team. Steve hung back until the crowd cleared, then made his way to the board. His name did not appear. "There must be some mistake," he thought and left to find the coach.

SAMPLE PASSAGE
FIRST PERSON POINT OF VIEW

My senior year has been awesome. I date the best looking girl in the class, my grades are above average, and I am going to be a starter on the basketball team. On my way to the gym, I think, "Life couldn't be better."

When I get to the gym, twenty guys are standing in front of the bulletin board, scanning the cut list for their names. I hear shouts of joy and sighs of pain as they learn whether or not they made the cut for the basketball team. I hang back until the guys clear out, then make my way to the board. My name is not on the list. I don't believe it. There must be some mistake. "Hey, Coach. Where are you?"

Minilesson 8

Skill
Maintaining a Personal Voice

Objective
Students will be able to recognize an author's voice, then reenter their rough drafts to clarify their voice.

Materials
Teacher: transparency of "Sample Passages Illustrating Voice"
construction paper
Student: rough draft
pen/pencil

Procedure
1. Explain voice to students:
"Each writer has a distinctive personality, and he or she possess a myriad of passions, facts, prejudices, and opinions. In writing, words must capture the writer's personality on the page for the reader. Writing with a strong voice will hold the reader's attention because of the individuality, liveliness, and energy it conveys. Strong voice also helps convey the purpose of the writing and aids the reader's ability to grasp the writer's ideas and emotions. Diction is another way a writer can convey his or her voice."
(See "Using Connotation for Diction" in Chapter Three)
2. Put "Sample Passages Illustrating Voice" on the overhead and read the first sample out loud with the students. Ask them,
"Does this author convey his or her voice? How does the reader know? (refer to the information in step 1) What can be inferred about the author of this piece?" (Possible responses could be patient and determined.)
Write the student's responses on the board. Read the second passage with the students and ask the same questions, writing their responses on the board. (Possible responses could be spontaneous and sense of humor.)
3. Ask students:
"Who is your intended audience? What voice would be most effective in communicating your message? Will you play the role of a friend hanging out at the mall or going to a movie, or a parent, lecturing, but doing what is right? Do you want to assume the role of a rival competing for the best, or an adver-

sary shouting in anger? When you determine the voice best suited to your purpose, write with that voice. Knowing your audience is the key to finding your voice."

Application
1. When students have made the decision about what voice they want to convey, instruct them to read their rough drafts, looking for passages, sentences, and/or words they can change. Ask them:
"How would you say this or tell this story to a friend, rival, parent, or adversary? What words would you use? What voice would you use?"
These questions will help them understand how to make the necessary revisions. If the minilessons on tone in this chapter and the minilesson on diction in Chapter Three have been taught, refer to them for additional help.
2. Divide the students into groups of three, and instruct each person to read his or her rough draft to the group. The listeners should help the reader identify areas that can and should be changed to allow the author's voice to be heard, then offer suggestions for revisions.
3. Allow time for the students to work individually, making the suggested revisions.

Assessment
1. When students have completed their revisions, instruct them to return to their groups. Then, instruct them to read their revisions and assess their effectiveness with the group. The group should determine which revision to share with the class, then write it on construction paper to post on the walls for other students to use as models.
2. After each group shares, ask the class to identify the voice and comment on its effectiveness.
3. A grade could be taken for group participation and/or completion of task.

Minilesson 8

Transparency

SAMPLE PASSAGE ILLUSTRATING VOICE

After waiting for what seemed like hours, I finally felt a bite on my line. I jumped up ready to do battle, grabbing my rod with both hands. The fish swam hard and fast, pulling too much line. I snapped my rod, pulling the line taut. The fish and I played tug of war, but the harder I pulled him toward the boat, the faster he swam away from it.

My body ached and my arms felt like jelly, but I was determined to win this battle. Just when I thought I couldn't pull anymore, the fish quit fighting. When I pulled that sucker out of the water, he looked awesome dangling from the end of my line. A thirteen pound black bass, the biggest fish I had ever caught.

I knew cutting class would get me in trouble, but I couldn't say no to the beautiful spring day. Taking chances was what I did best, and even if I did get busted, what could they do to me? Take away my birthday? I was already grounded for the rest of my life, so I had nothing to lose. Or so I thought.

My boyfriend Jerry and I left school after second period. We thought the mall a much better alternative than sitting in boring classes all day. We walked around the mall, looking in every store and wishing we had money to buy what we wanted. Just as we entered Foleys, we came face to face with the two people we had least expected to see, our mothers. Life as we knew it was over!

Minilesson 9

Skill
Adding Tone for Effect

Objective
Students will be able to identify tone, identify whether or not their rough drafts reflects tone, then reenter their rough drafts to determine what they are saying and how they are saying it.

Materials
Teacher: transparency of "Sample Passage Illustrating Tone"
3 x 5 cards
thesaurus for student use
butcher paper
markers
Students: rough draft
pen/pencil

Procedure
1. This lesson could take more than one 55 minute class period to teach; however, it could be adapted to fit that time frame or taught as is.
2. Write the definition of tone on the board, instructing students to copy the definition into their notebooks:

> Tone is a particular way of expressing feelings or attitudes that will influence how the reader feels about the characters, events, and outcome of the story.

> Speakers show tone more easily than writers because they can use voice tone, gesture, and facial expressions. A writer must use words alone.

3. Put "Sample Passages Illustrating Tone" on the overhead and read them with the class. Then ask:

> "What tone is conveyed in the first passage?" (tension, passion, fear, anxiety) "Second passage?" (sadness, longing, emptiness, grief) "Third passage?" (warmth, nostalgia, love, joyful)

4. Ask students:

> "What tools did the writers use to show tone?"

Write responses on the board, fitting the students' responses in the following categories and supplying the information students do not suggest. Students should write the following in their notebooks:

> Diction: individual words (see

"Using Connotation for Diction" in Chapter 3)

> Images: word pictures created by groups of words

> Details: facts–important to what is included, and to what is omitted

> Language: slang, scholarly, jargon

> Sentence Structure: short sentences are usually emotional or assertive; longer sentences are usually more reasonable or scholarly.

Application
1. Divide students into groups of three or four and give each group a 3 x 5 card with one of the following words written on it: *fear, hate, love, excitement, sadness, courage, anger, sympathy, tension, hysteria, boredom, anxiety, pride, happiness.* Hand out a thesaurus to each group and encourage the group to use it.
2. Instruct each group to write a description of someone walking down the hall of the school conveying the emotion or attitude on their card. The description must not contain the word on the card.
3. When the writing is complete, ask students to copy it with a marker on a piece of butcher paper and determine which tools (listed above in step 3) were used. Then, each group shares with the class, states the feeling or tone they conveyed, and notes the tools they used. The class will determine if the tone was conveyed effectively.
4. Invite students to read through their own rough drafts to determine its tone. Ask:

> "Did you convey tone in your piece? How do you know? What tone did you convey?"

5. Instruct students to highlight at least one sentence, paragraph, or dialog that needs to be rewritten in order to enhance or convey a certain tone.
6. Ask students to rewrite that section using the tools discussed.

Assessment
1. After rewriting, ask several students to write on a transparency the before and after passage they revised.
2. Read these with the class and ask them to assess the examples for effectiveness.

Minilesson 9

Transparency

SAMPLE PASSAGES ILLUSTRATING TONE

Tara bridled Smoke and led him out of the barn when a clap of thunder and a streak of lightning hit the ground. She turned to see Gulliver charging at her. Tara screamed so loudly her mother heard her in the house. Tara's mom jumped up and ran outside to find her. When she arrived at the stables, she found the fence broken and saw the horses running in the distance. Fear gripped her heart as she searched for her daughter.

I guess I knew the whole time Grandpa couldn't be helped, but I kept telling myself he was going to be fine. I wanted to believe he would live forever, but the cancer growing inside his body was stronger than his will to live. On a cold, dreary December morning, Grandpa drew his last breath.

My grandpa has been gone for six months now, and I still miss his big bear hugs, his funny stories, and his quiet laugh. People tell me my pain will go away and the memories will fade, but a part of me died with Grandpa. My life will never be the same.

My wide and curious eyes look up, and up, and up to meet the smiling face of my big brother. His crooked, gap-toothed grin and twinkling eyes gaze back at me, and he says, "Want to play?"

We pretend to drink tea and eat cookies; then he helps me feed my babies. When we are through, we run off, holding hands, to a make believe train going somewhere magical and amazing.

–Lisa Llano

Minilesson 10

Skill
Titles Perform a Function

Objective
Students will be able to recognize effective titles, then write an effective title with meaning.

Materials
Teacher: transparencies of two or three tables of contents from anthologies or magazines

class set of "Writing an Effective Title"

Student: rough draft
pen/pencil
notebook paper

Procedure
1. Ask students:

"How do you decide what selections to read in a short story anthology, magazine, or a poetry anthology?"

Write their responses on the board. Student selections are generally based on: title, length, and subject matter.

2. Explain to students:

"When a reader picks something to read based on the title, he or she expects the piece to relate to the title. This is why an effective title is so important. It should meet one or more of the following criteria:

accurately predicts the contents or focus of the piece (main idea)

sets limits on the topic

conveys the dominant impression the writer wants his or her piece to make

grabs the readers' attention by arousing their curiosity."

Application
1. Instruct students to fold a piece of paper in half, and on the top side, brainstorm a list of possible titles for their rough drafts using the criteria for an effective title. Encourage them to use as many of the suggestions as possible and to write the criteria used next to the possible title.

2. Then, instruct students to narrow their list of possible titles to one or two and hand out "Writing an Effective Title." Instruct students to revise their title, writing on the bottom half of the paper the technique they used and why they chose it.

Assessment
1. Ask every student to share his or her title and explain the choice.

2. The class gives feedback on each title's effectiveness based on the criteria written on the board.

Minilesson 10
Transparency

WRITING AN EFFECTIVE TITLE

1. Good titles usually involve a bit of word play by setting up a contrast. Choosing words with the same beginning sound helps to emphasize the contrast but is not always necessary.

    example: *Our Feast, Their Famine*

    Laugh All Day and Cry All Night

2. Use words in an unexpected way.

    example: *Try a Little Ardor*

    The Perils of Obedience

3. Sometimes a line or phrase heard or read will serve as a suitable title.

    example: *A Thousand Points of Light*

    The Party's Over

4. Try using alliteration in the title to catch the reader's attention.

    example: *Walk Through Winter*

    Seeds of Strength

5. Look for a phrase, repeated words, a quote, or idea used in the writing that might be a possible title.

6. Avoid using a question as a title. Remember the primary purpose of a title is to inform the reader.

7. A short phrase is better than a complete sentence, but if a short phrase is not enough, add a second phrase after a colon or vice versa.

    example: *Airlines: Still the Safest Way to Travel*

    Still the Safest Way to Travel: Airlines

8. Avoid using titles with an article followed by a noun or verb.

    example: *The Car*

    The Walk

    A Spring Day

Chapter 3

QUALITY WRITING HAS STYLE

Overview and Rationale

The minilessons in this chapter focus on the skills that add individual style to writing by using figurative language and varying sentence structure, thereby making it more interesting. When students apply these skills to their writing, the quality of their writing improves, and they recognize the improvement because they understand the skills.

These minilessons should be taught during the first semester because the skills relate to many of the grammar minilessons, and the application of these skills help increase the students' vocabulary. Also, since these skills provide students with the tools they need to elaborate, they score higher on writing assignments across the curriculum and on writing assessments.

Minilesson 11

Skill
Create Characters with Life

Objective
Students will be able to integrate grammar, literature, and writing in a way that will enable them to recognize quality characterization, then apply it in their own writing.

Materials
Student: class novel or short story
rough draft
pen/pencil
paper

Procedure
1. Instruct students to create a character grid by folding a piece of notebook paper in quarters lengthwise, then drawing a line down each fold and a line across the top. Write the word *adjectives* at the top of the first column, *nouns* in the second column, *adverbs* in the third column, and *verbs* in the last column. Model this grid by drawing it on the board.

2. Choose a character from a class novel or short story and complete the character grid with the students. As students choose adjectives, adverbs, nouns, and verbs relating to the character, write the words in the appropriate columns.

3. Explain:
"Characters become real people in the lives of the author who creates them, and a character must come alive for the readers in order for them to stay involved in the story."

Application
1. In order for students to see the connection between the characters in the novels they read and the characters they write about, place students in pairs and instruct them to exchange rough drafts with their partner. After reading their partner's story, instruct them to complete two character grids, one on each of the two main characters.

2. After returning the grids and rough drafts, the students should determine if the characters convey the characteristics they intended them to convey. Ask students,
"Do these words paint a true picture of the character? Do you know anyone in real life that fits this description?" If not, they need to deter

mine how they can revise their writing to make the character portrayal more accurate.

3. Instruct the students to make the necessary changes on the grid, then reenter their writing to find the most appropriate places to add or delete the information. Suggest using dialog.

4. After making the necessary revisions in their writing, students ask their partner to reread the story, noticing the revisions and determining if the changes had the desired effect.

Assessment
1. Each pair of students determines which revision they want to share with the class.

2. As students share, choose two to four examples to post on the wall for other students to use as models.

Minilesson 12

Skill
Elaboration Techniques That Work

Objective
Students will be able to recognize ways to elaborate, then apply the strategies learned in their writing.

Materials
Teacher: transparency of "Elboration"
            butcher paper
            colored markers
Student: rough draft
            pen/pencil

Procedure
1. Show students the "Elaboration" transparency, revealing only one line at a time.
2. Explain to students that we can also elaborate with words and write the following sentence on the board.
        The girl sang a song.
3. Ask students to elaborate this sentence by adding adjectives and adverbs.
        adjectives:
                What kind? (this could be written as a simile)
                Which one?
                 How many?
        adverbs:
                How?
                When did she sing?
                Where?
Adjectives and adverbs can be a:
        word: happily
        phrase: in the shower
        clause: while we were in the car

Application
1. Divide the students into groups of six. Each group has a leader, a scribe, and a task keeper.
2. Each group must elaborate the sentence, answering all six questions for adjectives and adverbs, then the scribe writes the sentence on the butcher paper provided.
3. Allow five to ten minutes for completion of the task; the task keeper makes sure the group finishes on time. The leader of each group shares the group's elaborated sentence and posts the butcher paper on the wall or board.

4. Point out that even though the sentences are not elaborated in the same way, they all extend the original sentence.
5. Instruct students to read their rough drafts and find a simple sentence that should be elaborated, then rewrite the sentence using this strategy.

Assessment
1. Ask students to share a "before and after" sentence with the class.
2. After each student shares, ask the class if the "after" sentence extends the writing. Be sure to probe for a rationale.

Contributed by Kathryn Yockstick

Minilesson 12

Transparency

ELABORATION

There once was a circle   E

Eyes to see   EL

Nose to smell   ELA

Mouth to eat   ELAB

Eyebrows for expression   ELABO

Eyelashes for protection   ELABOR

Hair for warm heads   ELABORA

Ears to hear   ELABORAT

Freckles added by sun   ELABORATI

Lines added by age   ELABORATIO

Smiles to show happiness   ELABORATION

Minilesson 13

Skill
Show, Don't Tell Using Imagery

Objective
Students will be able to recognize a telling sentence, then reenter their rough drafts and make that sentence a showing sentence with the use of imagery.

Materials
Teacher: poster board
colored markers
Student: rough draft
pen/pencil
highlighter
paper

Procedure
1. Explain:
"In order to make writing enjoyable to read, the writer must totally involve the reader. One way to accomplish this is to appeal to the reader's senses. If the reader can see and hear what is happening, and if he or she can smell and taste and touch what the characters experience, then the writer knows the writing is quality. Mark Twain said, "Don't tell me the old lady screamed, bring her on the stage and let me hear her scream." Write so a reader can hear the character scream.
2. Write the following sentence on the board.
The mugger attacked his victim.
3. Ask students:
"Does this sentence paint a picture for the reader? Are there details you could add to this sentence that would appeal to a reader's senses?"
4. Write the following suggestions on the board for specific ways students can revise by adding figurative language and imagery to their writing.
Use alliteration.
ex: *Slowly* and *silently* the mugger *stalked* his helpless victim.
Use a simile.
ex: When the moment arrived, he *struck as quick as a bull whip*, leaving the old woman motionless in the alley.
Use onomatopoeia.
ex: The bullet *whizzed* through the air, striking the victim with deadly force.
Use a metaphor.
ex: *The mugger, a panther in the night,* running through the streets from his past.
5. Write the following telling sentences on the board and instruct students to rewrite two of the three using figurative language. Challenge the students to write the showing sentences without using the italicized words. This will greatly extend their vocabularies.
The *fight* at school today was *unbelievable.*
The *cheerleaders* think they are so good.
Our *cafeteria food* is *awful.*
6. Allow five minutes for students to work, then ask several to share what they wrote.

Application
1. Ask students to read their rough drafts to a partner. The partner will listen for telling sentences which are often signaled by the use of *be* verbs: *am, is, are, was, were, be, being, been.*
2. When telling sentences have been discovered, the author highlights them, then rewrites them using the models demonstrated.

Assessment
1. Ask students to share one sentence before and after they revised it.
2. The class chooses three or four of the revisions to rewrite on a poster board to post on the wall for other students to use as models.

Minilesson 14

Skill
Show Don't Tell Using Reporter's Formula

Objective
Students will be able to recognize a telling sentence, then reenter their rough draft and write a showing sentence using reporter's formula.

Materials
Teacher: poster board
colored markers
Student: rough draft
pen/pencil
highlighter
paper

Procedure
1. Write the following sentence on the board:

John is working hard.

2. Ask students:

"Does this sentence paint a picture for the reader? Does this sentence leave questions in the reader's mind? Does it answer the questions who, what, when, where, why, how? How could this sentence answer these questions and, at the same time, paint a picture for the reader?"

3. Answer each question about this sentence.

Who is John?
i.e. a seventeen-year-old student
What does he do at work?
i.e. stocks and sacks groceries
When does he work?
i.e. after school and weekends
Where does he work?
i.e. Albertson's grocery store
Why does he work?
i.e. saving money for a car and insurance
How does he work?
i.e. hard

4. Instruct students to rewrite this sentence, showing the reader a picture of John with words.

John, a seventeen-year-old student, comes home exhausted from Albertson's after stocking countless cans of vegetables on shelves and sacking an endless number of carts full of groceries for customers with crying babies and bad attitudes. He knows driving the sleek, red Corvette will be worth all of the hours he sacrificed after school and on weekends.

5. Write the following telling sentences on the board and instruct students to rewrite them using reporter's formula.

Sarah is a dancer.
Todd is a jock.

6. Allow five minutes for students to work, then ask several to share their revisions.

Application
1. Ask students to read their rough drafts to a partner. The partner will listen for telling sentences which are often signaled by the use of *be* verbs: *am, is, are, was, were, be, being, been.*

2. When telling sentences have been discovered, the author highlights them, then rewrites them using reporter's formula.

Assessment
1. Ask students to share one sentence before and after they revised it.

2. The class chooses three or four of the revisions to rewrite on a poster board to post on the wall for other students to use as models.

Minilesson 15

Skill
Using Dialog Appropriately

Objective
Students will be able to determine when to use dialog and how to write it effectively. Then they reenter their rough drafts to determine where to add dialog or how to revise the dialog they have written.

Materials
Teacher: art transparencies or posters depicting people
Student: rough draft
pen/pencil
notebook paper

Procedure
1. Explain:

"Dialog is a conversation between two or more people, and in fiction writing it is essential. Think about how dialog allows the reader to enjoy reading. The dialog brings the characters to life and adds interest to the story. But for dialog to perform that function, it must do more than duplicate real speech. Real people have dull conversations like:

"Hi, how are you?"
"I'm fine. How about you?"
"I'm fine, but in a hurry."
"See you later. I'm on my way to class."
"Okay. Have a good day."

Quality dialog in fiction has been put through a strainer, and only the most interesting, most exciting, most emotional, and most dramatic words come through the strainer."

2. To motivate students to think about using dialog, ask them to brainstorm people that could have a conversation and write their responses on the board.

ex: parent–child
teacher–student

3. Ask students what type of things these pairs could talk about.

ex: parent–child:
curfew, dating, clothes, money
teacher–student:
grades, tardies, tests, detention

4. Divide the students into pairs and show them a poster or art transparency depicting people. Ask them to use their imagination to invent a situation between the people in the picture and write a dialog of at least ten lines, dropping the listener into the middle of the conversation. Encourage students to make an effort to go beyond the words *said* and *asked* in their dialog tag, using some explanatory material.

5. Write the following functions for dialog on the board:

Provide information
Describe a place or character
Create a sense of time
Reveal a character's thoughts
Move the story forward
Summarize what has happened
Create a sense of place
Create conflict or suspense

Application
1. Ask students to read their rough drafts, looking for places they can add dialog. Remind them to look at the list on the board to help them find passages that could be livened up with quality dialog. Add the following idea to the list:

Telling about a conversation
(indirect dialog)
ex: I told her that he wouldn't go
with me.

2. Explain to students that the use of a dialog tag is not always necessary. If two people are having a conversation, and it is clear to the reader who is talking, then omit the dialog tag. Relate this to their own reading by asking them if they always read the dialog tags.

3. To help students revise dialog they have already written, instruct them to cover their dialog with their finger one line at a time. Then, read the dialog without the covered line. If the story line makes sense without the covered line, change or eliminate the dialog.

Assessment
1. Ask several students to read the dialog they added, explain why they added it, and tell what function it serves.

2. Ask several students to read dialog before and after they revised it and explain why they made the revision.

3. Ask several students to read dialog before and after they eliminated the dialog tags.

Minilesson 16

Skill
Using Connotation for Diction

Objective
The students will be able to identify synonyms that have different connotations, then reenter their rough drafts to add or change words conveying the most appropriate meaning in context.

Materials
Teacher: word lists on 3 x 5 cards
         10 - 12 dictionaries
         10 - 12 thesauri
Student: rough draft
        pen/pencil
        highlighter

Procedure
1. Divide the class into groups of three or four and give each group one of the following lists of words that have the similar meanings:

1. friendly	2. beautiful	3. fear
sociable	lovely	dread
neighborly	exquisite	terror
cheerful	good-looking	panic
effervescent	pretty	apprehension
congenial	attractive	anxiety
4. walk	5. fat	6. eat
march	obese	nibble
saunter	chubby	devour
amble	stout	pig-out
stroll	plump	gobble
hike	stocky	chow down
7. friend	8. fight	9. shy
buddy	brawl	demure
companion	quarrel	timid
acquaintance	altercation	coy
colleague	fray	reserved
playmate	dispute	bashful

2. Have groups label each word on their list as positive, +; negative, -; or neutral, o; with the appropriate symbol. Most words can be positive, negative, or neutral depending on the context they choose. Then choose two words to demonstrate to the class by a skit or drawing.

3. Each group will then tell the word and its meaning and present a demonstration of the words they chose.

4. The class will then state the difference in feeling or connotation of the words demonstrated.

5. Explain:

     "Words having the same general meaning often bring out different feelings or attitudes. Diction, or individual word choice, helps convey tone by the connotations the word suggests."

Write the following definitions on the board:
Connotation–to suggest certain meanings in addition to explicit meanings.
Diction–includes language and figurative language, word choice by the author that promotes the tone of the piece of writing.

Application
1. Next, using a thesaurus, students read through their rough drafts looking for words that could be replaced with words having stronger connotative meanings to help them convey the tone of their rough drafts. Each student or pair of students will need a thesaurus and a dictionary.

2. Look for the words *said, nice, walk, run, little, big, good, bad, happy*, or *sad* and replace them with words that have stronger connotative meaning.

3. Instruct students to highlight the word or words they wish to change, then write the new word above the highlighted one.

Assessment
1. Ask students to share one revision they made with the class.

2. As they share, have a student to write both words on the board and leave them there as models for other classes.

Minilesson 17

Skill
Varying Sentence Patterns and Lengths

Objective
The students will be able to recognize the length and pattern of the sentences they write, then reenter their rough drafts to make the necessary revisions.

Materials
Teacher: transparency of "Sample Passage without Varied Sentence Patterns and Lengths"
class set of "Suggested Ways to Vary Sentence Patterns and Lengths"
blank transparencies
3 different colors of transparency pens
Student: rough draft
pen/pencil
2 different color highlighters

Procedure
1. Explain:
"One way to hold the reader's attention is to vary sentence patterns and lengths. Writing the same length and pattern of sentences makes writing dull and reading monotonous."

On the overhead, show students the transparency "Sample Passage without Varied Sentence Patterns or Lengths".

2. Read the passage with the students, then model the following procedure on the transparency. First, underline the sentences in alternating colors. Students will see immediately if the sentences are the same length or if there are too many long or short sentences.

3. Hand out the list of "Suggested Techniques to Vary Sentence Patterns and Lengths" and encourage students to make suggestions for revising the sentences in the passage.

4. When the revision is complete, write the revised passage on a transparency and underline the sentences in alternating colors. Students will notice that revising the sentence patterns usually altered the sentence lengths. Read the passage so students hear how much better the revised passage sounds.

Application
1. Instruct the students to read through their rough drafts, revising sentences for length and patterns using the suggestions on the handout. Require students to make a determined number of changes, based on the length of their rough drafts and time in class to work.

2. Circulate the room to assist students in their revision.

Assessment
1. Ask several students to read their before and after passage. Discuss with students the positive changes their revision made.

2. Ask the students to determine the most effective revision and write it with the original on a transparency to use as a model.

Minilesson 17

Transparency

Sample Passage Without Varied Sentence Patterns and Lengths

My slumber party was a blast! We ran out of food around 12:30 AM. All we wanted was more Dr. Pepper and chips and getting them became our mission. The store was too far away for us to walk to, and the car sat idly in the garage. My friends and I decided to take a risk. We jumped in the car and began our two mile trek to the store. We arrived safely, and purchased our goodies. We returned home with no problems. But Mom was waiting for us in the driveway. Mom was madder than I had ever seen her. She told us to get out of the car, and we promptly obeyed. I was more scared at that moment than I had ever been. I was more embarrassed than scared. Mom took away our food, and she made my friends call their parents to come and pick them up.

Minilesson 17

Transparency/Handout

SUGGESTED TECHNIQUES TO VARY SENTENCE PATTERN AND LENGTHS

1. Use one of the following subordinate conjunctions to combine two sentences showing the relationship between two ideas: *after, although, as, because, before, if, since, than, that, though, unless, until, when, where, or while.*

example: My slumber party was a blast! We ran out of food around 12:30 AM.
revision: My slumber party was a blast <u>until</u> we ran out of food around 12:30AM.

2. Add a phrase beginning with an infinitive.

example: All we wanted was more Dr. Pepper and chips and getting them became our mission.
revision: <u>To get</u> more Dr. Pepper and chips became our mission.

3. Write one compound sentence—two sentences joined with a comma and one of the coordinating conjunctions (FANBOYS is a mnemonic for: *For, And, Nor, But, Or, Yet, So*).

example: The store was too far away for us to walk<u>, yet</u> the car sat idly in the garage.

4. Change a statement to a question.

example: My friends and I decided to take a risk.
revision: My friends and I looked at one another and silently asked, <u>"Should we take a risk?"</u>

5. Add a phrase beginning with a present participle, a verbal that ends in *ing*.

example: We jumped in the car and began our two mile trek to the store.
revision: <u>Nodding our heads in agreement</u>, we jumped in the car and began our two mile trek   to the store.

6. Add an adverb clause, a dependent clause beginning with the subordinating conjunctions listed in number 1.

example: We arrived safely and purchased our goodies. We returned home with no problems.
revision: <u>After we purchased our goodies</u>, we returned home with no problems.

7. Add an adjective clause, a dependent clause beginning with relative pronouns: which, that, whom, whose, or who.

example: But Mom was waiting for us in the driveway. She was angrier than I had ever seen her.
revision: But waiting for us in the driveway stood Mom, <u>who was angrier than I had ever see her</u>.

8. Add dialog.

example: She told us to get out of the car...
revision: She yelled, <u>"Get out of that car. Now!"</u>

9. Start with an *ly* word.

example: ...and, we promptly obeyed.
revision: <u>Quickly,</u> we obeyed.

10. Start one sentence with a prepositional phrase.

example: I was more scared at that moment than I had ever been.
revision: <u>At that moment,</u> I was more scared than I had ever been.

4

TEACH GRAMMAR THROUGH REVISION

Overview and Rationale

Grammar is the heart of writing because if writing is not grammatically correct, it affects the reader's ability to understand what the author is saying. Grammar is also what students dislike the most, partly because they are taught the same skills year after year, and partly because of the way the skills are taught. Rote memorization of parts of speech and grammar rules does not capture the interest of teenagers. The information has no relevance to them, and it does not transfer to the long term memory of the brain (Sousa 16).

Research shows that today's students do not learn grammar in isolation, and secondary English teachers prove it to themselves every year. They know subjects and verbs are taught in elementary school, but they have secondary students in their classrooms that cannot identify them in a sentence.

The time for change is now. Teaching grammar in the context of a student's writing and using the grammar book as a resource produces students comfortable and knowledgeable about the proper use of the English language. The minilessons in this chapter show how to effectively teach grammar within the context of a student's writing in a way that students will learn and apply the skills.

The rules and lists used in this chapter can be enlarged on a poster machine. If a poster of the rules and lists are kept up throughout the year, students can easily refer to them when they write, revise, and edit.

Minilesson 18

Skill
Changing Past Tense Verbs to Present Tense

Objective
The students will recognize and understand the power of the present tense and learn to write in the present tense, then reenter their rough drafts, changing past tense verbs to present tense.

Materials
Teacher: transparency of "Sample Passages Written in Past Tense" (top half for guided practice)

1 copy of the lower passage for every student

Student: rough draft
pen/pencil
highlighter

Procedure
1. Write the following examples on the board:

ex: Sherry saw her boyfriend at Lucy's locker, and her anger flared. She marched over to them, pushed Lucy into the wall, and screamed at her.

ex: Sherry sees her boyfriend at Lucy's locker and her anger flares. She marches over to them, pushes Lucy into the wall, and screams at her.

2. Read the sentences out loud with the students, then ask them,

"Which passage involves the reader's emotion? Why?"

Explain to students:

"Present tense verbs are happening now and they drop the reader into the middle of the action."

3. Put the transparency "Sample Passages Written in Past Tense" on the overhead, covering the passage you copied for the students. Read the passage with the students, then with the students' help, underline all the past tense verbs.

4. Next, revise the passage with the students, changing the past tense verbs to present tense. This is an appropriate time to review past tense: action which is completed at a particular time in the past. Not all verbs can be changed to past tense.

5. Give each student a copy of the second passage. Instruct them to highlight the verbs, then change them from past to present tense.

6. Circulate the room to check for understanding.

7. Put the passage on the overhead and ask the students to share their revisions. Change the verbs on the transparency, then read the revised passage together.

Application
1. Instruct students to underline the past tense verbs in their rough drafts, then change them to present tense. Also, challenge them to use stronger, more vivid verbs, making their writing more powerful.

2. Circulate the room to help students individually.

Assessment
Ask each student to share one revision they made.

Minilesson 18

Transparency

SAMPLE PASSAGES WRITTEN IN PAST TENSE

I looked down on Fifth Avenue in New York City from my hotel room window and noticed it was alive with activity. Horns honked and tires squealed as cars sped down the busy thoroughfare. Pulsating throngs of people pushed and shoved their way to work, glaring at one another. Street vendors sold hotdogs and ice cream of every variety, and corner musicians played their songs for any-one who listened. Both worked for a meager existence. Teenagers skated among the people, bumping and hitting anyone in their path. One young skater knocked an old man down, but no one stopped to help him to his feet. I wondered if the people on the street ever took the time to smell the roses.

I glanced down the cliff and imagined falling to my death. I shuddered and continued to walk along the path, trying to watch my every step. Suddenly, I slipped on some loose rocks and felt myself falling down the cliff. I reached and grabbed for anything I could to stop my fall, but I came up with air. Luckily, my jacket caught on the limb of a tree. I rested there until I heard a loud crack and felt the branch begin to give away. I screamed like a wild banshee, hoping someone would hear me. Fear rushed through me like a bolt of lightning as the branch broke with a loud snap. I fell down the cliff and pain seared through my body. Rocks jabbed my sides and cut my arms and legs. When I finally stopped, a cloud of blackness came over me.

Minilesson 19

Skill
Making Subjects and Present Tense Verbs Agree

Objective
Students will be able to identify subjects and verbs and determine their number, then reenter their rough drafts to check for subject/verb agreement.

Materials
Teacher: transparencies
           transparency pens
           poster of "Rules for Subject and
                Present Tense Verb Agreement"
Student: rough draft
           pen/pencil
           paper
           2 colors of highlighters

Procedure
1. Explain to students the rules for subject and present tense verb agreement and put up the poster.

2. Instruct the students to write the rules in their notebooks for later reference.

3. Model the rules by asking students to share sentences from their rough drafts. Write the sentences on a transparency.

4. After you have written four to six sentences, ask students to identify the subject and verb in each sentence, underlining the correct response.

5. Next, ask students to refer to the rules to check for agreement. Then ask them to state the rule that validates their answer.

6. Repeat steps 4 and 5 until there is a general understanding.

Application
1. Instruct students to highlight all subjects in one color and all verbs in another in their rough drafts.

2. Circulate the room to answer questions as they arise. Students finishing quickly can help those that need additional help.

3. Instruct students to fold a piece of notebook paper in quarters lengthwise so they have four columns; number the columns 1, 2, 3, and 4.

4. Students will then list the subjects they highlighted in column 1 and the verbs corre-sponding to those subjects on the same line in column 2. When columns 1 and 2 are full, they will continue their lists in columns 3 and 4.

5. After listing all of the subjects and verbs, they can easily identify the ones that do not agree. Then they must change either the subject or the verb to make them agree.

6. Repeat step 2.

Assessment
1. In small groups, instruct the students to exchange their subject/verb lists and check for agreement.

2. Ask students to share the changes they made with the class.

Minilesson 19

Transparency/Poster

RULES FOR SUBJECT AND PRESENT TENSE VERB AGREEMENT

A verb must agree in number, singular or plural, with its subject.

If the subject is singular, its verb must be singular.

example: She walks.

If the subject is plural, its verb must be plural.

example: The girls walk.

The singular form of a regular verb ends in -s; the plural form of the verb does not.

Minilessons for Revision–©1997 Absey & Co., 23011 Northcrest, Spring, Texas 77389, 281.257.2340

Minilesson 20

Skill
Eliminating Sentence Fragments

Objective
Students will be able to identify sentence fragments in their writing, then rewrite the sentence correctly.

Materials
Teacher: poster of "Guidelines for Complete Sentences"
Student: rough draft
pen/pencil
fine line markers

Procedure
1. Post "Guidelines for Complete Sentences" and instruct students to write them in their notebooks.

2. Next, instruct students to circle the subject and verb of each sentence in the same color in which it is underlined (see minilesson 17).

3. Illicit several sentences that model each rule and write them on the board or a transparency.

4. Ask students to find sentences in their rough drafts that do not fit one of the patterns. Write them on the board and explain their structure. Further explanation will be necessary for sentences that contain dependent clauses. (see "Combining Sentences" in this chapter)

Application
1. Instruct students to look carefully at each sentence, making sure it has at least one subject and one verb and expresses at least one complete thought.

2. Ask students to find a fragment, a sentence that does not meet the above criteria, and rewrite the sentence correctly.

3. Circulate the room to help students individually.

Assessment
1. Instruct students to exchange their rough drafts with a partner to double check for sentence fragments.

2. Ask students to share a sentence they corrected.

Minilesson 20
Transparency/Poster

GUIDELINES FOR COMPLETE SENTENCES

- **Traditionally, sentences must have at least one subject and one verb and express at least one complete thought.**

    example: Kevin planned a Halloween party for his friends.

    A dependent clause has a subject and verb, but it does not express a complete thought.

    example: While Kevin planned a Halloween Party for his friends

- **A complete sentence can have two subjects and one verb.**

    example: Sally and her friends wanted to wear costumes.

- **A complete sentence can have one subject and two verbs.**

    example: Kevin arranged a contest and bought prizes for the winners.

- **Traditional compound sentences are two simple sentences joined with a coordinating conjunction—FANBOYS—and can have any combination of subjects and verbs listed above in the simple sentences.**

    example: The high school art teacher and the local theater director agreed to be the judges for Kevin's costume contest, *and* they would choose the winners and award the prizes.
    subject, subject, verb, and subject, verb, verb

    example: Kevin offered to pay them for their time, *but* they declined any payment.
    subject, verb, but subject, verb

    example: The costumes were awesome, *and* Sally and her friends won first place.
    subject, verb, and subject, subject, verb

Minilesson 21

Skill
Revising Adverbs and Weak Verbs into Powerful Verbs

Objective
Students will be able to identify adverbs, then find examples of them in their rough drafts, eliminating the adverb by changing the verb to a stronger one.

Materials
Teacher: dictionary and thesaurus for student use
    half sheets of colored paper
Student: rough draft
    pen/pencil
    highlighter

Procedure
1. Define adverb and instruct students to write the definition in their notebooks:
    An adverb answers the questions how, when, where, how often, and to what extent about the word or phrase it modifies which can be a verb, an adjective, or another adverb.
2. Instruct students to highlight the adverbs and the words they modify.
3. Circulate about the room to offer individual help.
4. Ask students for examples of sentences containing adverbs used as modifiers from their rough drafts and write the adverb and the word it modifies on the board.
5. Solicit from the class how to eliminate the adverbs used to modify verbs in the examples on the board. Ask students what question each adverb is answering. This should help them come up with stronger verbs.
    ex: Jennifer *proudly walked* across the stage to receive her diploma. (answers how?)
    revision: Jennifer *strutted* across the stage to receive her diploma.
    ex: Her parents *were very proud* of her achievement. (answers to what extent?) very is not necessary
6. Solicit from the class how to eliminate the adverbs used to modify adjectives in the examples on the board.
    ex: The graduation party was *relatively small.* (answers to what extent) relatively

is not necessary
    ex: Everyone present had an *extremely good* time. (answers to what extent)
    revision: Everyone had a blast! (replace adverb, adjective, and noun with one strong noun)

Application
1. Working in pairs, instruct the students to find, then change the weak verb strings in their writing to stronger, more specific ones with the help of a dictionary and thesaurus.
2. Instruct students to *X* out the words *very*, *really*, and *a lot.* Students may need to replace the word with a more descriptive noun, verb, or adjective.

Assessment
1. Ask each student to share one example of a sentence he or she revised with the class.
2. Give each student a half sheet of colored paper to write his or her best revision, then post them for other classes to use as models.

Minilesson 22

Skill
Writing with Specific Nouns

Objective
Students will be able to recognize vague nouns, then replace them in their rough drafts with more specific and particular nouns.

Materials
Teacher: sheets of colored paper
Students: rough draft
　　　　　pen/pencil
　　　　　highlighter

Procedure
1. Explain to students:

"More specific and particular nouns are better because they show, not tell. Quality writing is clear and specific, not vague.

ex: The *flowers* in the *field* bloom every spring.

revision: The *bluebonnets* on *Interstate 35* bloom every spring."

2. Abstract nouns like love, joy, anger, fear, and courage tell; they do not show.

ex: Jeff was angry at his sister.

revision: Jeff screamed at his sister, then slammed the door to her room as he stomped out.

3. Ask:

"In the revised sentence, what emotion is Jeff feeling? (anger) How do you know? Does the author tell you?"

Application
1. Divide students in pairs and instruct them to read his or her rough drafts to one another, listening for vague nouns and highlighting them.

2. After both partners have read, each author revises his or her sentences changing the vague nouns to a more specific ones.

Assessment
1. After the revisions have been made, students share with their partner.

2. Each pair should pick two revisions and share with the class.

3. Ask several students to write their before and after sentences on colored paper to post in the room.

Minilesson 23

Skill
Writing with Strong Verbs

Objective
Students will be able to identify weak verb structures in their writing, then reenter their rough drafts to make the verbs more powerful.

Materials
Teacher: poster board of "Guidelines for Powerful Verbs"
sentence strips
Student: rough draft
pen/pencil
highlighter
paper

Procedure
1. Explain:
   "Verbs are the power source in sentences. Without them the sentence has no life and the story has no action."
2. As you explain the guidelines for using powerful verbs, post them and the list of *be* verbs and instruct students to write the rules in their notebooks.
3. Next, instruct students to highlight all verbs and verb structures in their rough drafts.
   ex: The day *was simmering* hot.
   Although the heat *was unbearable*, we *continued* the picnic.
   The heat *intensified* later in the day.
4. Circulate the room to help students. Students finishing quickly can help those needing additional help.

Application
Instruct each student to find sentences in his or her rough draft that model an example of a broken guideline, then revise them to fit the appropriate guideline.

Assessment
1. Instruct the students to pick the revised sentence they think is the best and write it on a sentence strip.
2. As students share their revised sentences, instruct them to put the sentence strips up in the room for other students to use as models.

Minilesson 23

Transparency/Poster

GUIDELINES FOR POWERFUL VERBS

- **Powerful verbs show, not tell.**

    example: She <u>walked</u> through the hall.

    She <u>groped</u> her way through the hall.

    example: Sally <u>drove</u> down the deserted highway.

    Sally <u>sped</u> down the deserted highway.

- **Single verbs are stronger than verbs and adverbs.**

    example: The snake <u>slowly moved</u> through the grass.

    The snake <u>slithered</u> through the grass.

    example: Darcy <u>quickly ran</u> down the stairs.

    Darcy <u>fled</u> down the stairs.

- **Limit using have/had/has combined with nouns.**

    example: They <u>had</u> a big <u>fight</u> in the hall.

    They <u>fought</u> in the hall.

- **Limit using "to be" verbs: am, is, are, was, were, be, being, been**

    example: She <u>is eating</u> lunch quickly.

    She <u>gobbles</u> down her lunch.

    example: Justin <u>was</u> quietly <u>laughing</u> at the joke.

    Justin <u>chuckled</u> at the joke.

- **Limit using a noun that could be a verb.**

    example: We had a <u>disagreement</u>.

    We <u>disagreed</u>. (argued, fought)

    example: Mindy went for a <u>ride</u> in the car.

    Mindy <u>rode</u> in the car.

Minilessons for Revision–©1997 Absey & Co., 23011 Northcrest, Spring, Texas 77389, 281.257.2340

Minilesson 24

Skill
Using Pronouns and Antecedents Correctly

Objective
Students will be able to recognize pronouns and their corresponding antecedents, then check for correct use of this grammatical concept by reentering their rough drafts.

Materials
Teacher: poster of "Pronouns"
Student: rough draft
            pen/pencil
            highlighter

Procedure
1. Post the poster and explain the function for each type of pronoun. Instruct students to write the pronouns in their notebooks.

2. Instruct the students to highlight the listed pronouns in their rough drafts. (This lesson could be divided into two lessons.)

3. Circulate the room to help students. Students finishing quickly can help those needing additional guidance.

Application
1. Instruct the students to replace the second person pronouns, you, your, and yours, with a more appropriate word unless it is used in dialog or they want to address the reader—use sparingly and carefully.
        ex: When *you* take drugs, *you* will suffer the consequences.
        revision: Taking drugs can cause serious consequences.

2. Write the definition of an antecedent on the board and instruct the students to write it in their notebooks:
        An antecedent is the word to which the pronoun refers.

3. Instruct the students to draw an arrow from the pronoun to the noun to which it refers.
        ex: Jason takes medication before *he* comes to school.

4. Students will be able to see if a pronoun has too many antecedents by the number of arrows they draw to one noun. If a noun has too many arrows drawn to it, students will need to replace some of the pronouns for clarity. For example, when Mary is mentioned in the first sentence, and not again throughout the narra-

tive, the need for clarity will be obvious.

5. If a pronoun has no corresponding antecedent, instruct students to correct the problem by adding an appropriate antecedent. In some cases the sentence may need to be rewritten or combined.

6. Circulate about the room to help students.

Assessment
1. Divide the students into groups of three to evaluate their revisions.

2. Ask students to share their revisions with the class.

Minilesson 24
Transparency/Poster

PRONOUNS

	SUBJECT	OBJECT
Singular:	I, he, she, it, you	me, him, her, it
Plural:	we, they, you	us, them

REFLEXIVE

Singular: myself, herself, himself

Plural: ourselves, themselves

POSSESSIVE

Singular: my, mine, his, hers, its, your, yours

Plural: our, ours, their, theirs, your, yours

INDEFINITE

Singular: each, either, neither, one, everybody, everyone, everything, someone, somebody, anybody, anything, nobody, another

Plural: both, several, many, few

Both Singular and Plural: all, any, half, most, none, some

Minilessons for Revision–©1997 Absey & Co., 23011 Northcrest, Spring, Texas 77389, 281.257.2340

Minilesson 25

Skill
Making Pronouns and Antecedents Agree

Objective
Students will be able to identify pronouns and their corresponding antecedents, then check for agreement in number and gender.

Materials
Teacher: poster of "Pronouns" (from "Using Pronouns and Antecedents Correctly")

poster of "Pronoun and Antecedents"

Student: rough draft

pen/pencil

highlighter

paper

Procedure
1. Review the types of pronouns written on the poster, then instruct students to highlight all of the pronouns in their rough drafts. If they are working on the same rough drafts they used for the pronoun/antecedent lesson, this step should be omitted.

2. Instruct students to fold a sheet of paper in quarters lengthwise so they will have four columns, then number the columns 1, 2, 3, and 4.

3. Instruct the students to list their pronouns in column 1, and the corresponding antecedents in column 2. When columns 1 and 2 are full, students continue their lists in columns 3 and 4.

4. Post the rules for agreement and explain them to the students. Ask students to write the rules in their notebooks.

Application
1. Instruct students to look at their list and check the pronouns and antecedents for agreement in gender and number using the rules posted.

2. If they find a problem in agreement, have them revise their rough drafts to make pronouns and antecedents agree.

3. Circulate the room to help students. Students finishing quickly can help those needing guidance.

Assessment
1. Pair up the students and ask them to exchange lists, making sure all agreement problems were found and corrected.

2. Ask each student to share a change he or she made.

Minilesson 25

Transparency/Poster

PRONOUNS AND ANTECEDENTS

- **A singular pronoun must correspond to a singular antecedent.**

  example: The *athlete* left school early so *she* could get to the game on time.

- **A plural pronoun must refer to a plural antecedent.**

  example: The *athletes* left school early so *they* could get to the game on time.

- **Pronouns that refer to a male or female must correspond to the correct gender.**

  example: *Jason* scored a touchdown before *he* broke his leg.
  Jennifer left the party when *she* saw Tom kiss Sue.

- **An antecedent is the word to which the pronoun refers.**

Minilesson 26

Skill
Using *be* Verbs Sparingly

Objective
Students will be able to recognize *be* verbs in their writing, then replace them using a variety of methods.

Materials
Teacher: poster of "Strategies for Eliminating *be* Verbs"
        butcher paper
        colored markers
Student: rough draft
        pen/pencil
        highlighter

Procedure
1. Write the *be* verbs on the board: *am, is, are, was, were, be, being, been.*

2. Explain:

"Using too many *be* verbs makes your writing weak and dull to read and is also a sign of an immature writer. So, in order to make your writing livelier, you are going to eliminate some of those weak *be* verbs."

3. Instruct students to highlight all of the *be* verbs in their rough drafts (with the exception of those in dialog), count them, and put the number at the top of their rough drafts.

NOTE: If students have no *be* verbs because they used unnecessary or conversational dialog, instruct them to rewrite their rough drafts, using explanatory material and less dialog.

4. Ask for examples of sentences from students' rough drafts with *be* verbs and write them on the board. Model how they can be changed using "Strategies for Eliminating *be* Verbs."

NOTE: Do not sacrifice structure and meaning to eliminate a *be* verb. Sometimes they are the only verbs that work.

Application
1. Instruct students to eliminate half of the *be* verbs in their rough drafts using the strategies. As students become proficient in this exercise, they will quit using unnecessary *be* verbs in their rough drafts.

2. Circulate the room to answer questions and offer help. Students understanding this concept can help those needing guidance.

Assessment
1. In large or small groups, ask each student to share one sentence, reading the original sentence first, then the revision.

2. Write some of the best revisions on butcher paper for other classes to use as models.

Minilesson 26

Transparency/Poster

STRATEGIES FOR ELIMINATING *BE* VERBS

- **Change the *be* verb to a stronger, livelier verb.**

    example: She *is unwilling* to clean her room.
    revision: She *refuses* to clean her room.

- **Eliminate the *be* verb by writing one or more *showing* sentences.**

    example: Her room *is* a mess.
    revision: Susan's room has clothes *piled* in the corner, dirty dishes hidden under the bed, papers scattered on the floor, and dust an inch thick covering the furniture.

- **Combine the sentence with the one before or after it using a phrase or a clause.**

    example: When I *was* six, I went to the circus. I *was thrilled* at what I saw.
    revision: At the age of six, going to my first circus *thrilled* me.

- **Leave it alone if changing it would diminish or change the meaning or create awkward structure.**

- **Omit the sentence.**

Minilesson 27

Skill
Using Passive and Active Voice Correctly

Objective
Students will be able to identify the passive voice in their writing, then change it to the active voice when appropriate.

Materials
Teacher: poster of "Passive and Active Voice"
Student: rough draft
   pen/pencil
   highlighter

Procedure
1. Explain and post "Passive and Active Voice."

2. Ask students to copy the information in their notebooks.

3. Instruct students to read their rough drafts with a partner in order to identify the sentences written in passive voice. Remind them to listen for *be* verbs and highlight passive verb structures when they read them.

4. Circulate the room to help students.

5. Ask students for sentences they found with passive voice and write them on the board. Model for students how the sentences can be written in active voice.

6. For reinforcement of this concept, see "Writing with Strong Verbs"and "Using *be* Verbs Sparingly."

Application
1. Using the poster, instruct the pairs of students to rewrite the sentences that need to be changed from passive to active voice.

2. Circulate about the room to help students.

Assessment
1. Join two pairs of students to make groups of four and ask the students to share their revisions with the group.

2. Join each group to hear the revisions.

Minilesson 27

Transparency/Poster

PASSIVE AND ACTIVE VOICE

The voice of the verb lets the reader know if the subject is doing the action or receiving the action.

- **When the subject receives the action or is not personally doing the action, the voice is passive. Passive voice is generally wordier.**

  Note: When changing passive voice to active, the object of the preposition becomes the subject.

  example: The pizza *was eaten* by the boys.
  example: The class *was dismissed* by the teacher.

- **When the subject performs the action; the voice is active. Active voice is preferred because it is more direct and concise.**

  example: The boys *ate* the pizza.
  example: The teacher *dismissed* the class.

- **Active voice makes the writing more interesting.**

- **Passive voice is usually weak and easy to recognize because of the *be* verb.**

Minilesson 28

Skill
Combining Sentences

Objective
Students will be able to identify simple sentences in their rough drafts, then combine them with other sentences in their rough drafts, making their writing clearer and more concise.

Materials
Teacher: blank transparencies
　　　　　transparency pens
　　　　　transparency of "Sentence Combining Practice"
　　　　　class set of "Techniques Used to Combine Sentences"
Student: rough draft
　　　　　pen/pencil
　　　　　highlighter
　　　　　notebook paper

Procedure
1. Explain:

"Combining sentences is necessary in order to make your writing more interesting to read. Changing the arrangement of words, phrases, and clauses in your sentences allows you to create energy, vary meaning, and establish emphasis. Combining sentences can also make the writing easier to understand and more concise."

2. Put the students into pairs, then place the transparency "Sentence Combining Practice" on the overhead, covering the revision, and instruct students to combine the sentences.

3. Ask each group to share their revision with the class. After each group has shared, point out that there are many ways sentences can be combined, depending on the author's style or the given context. One way is not better than the other, but creating apt, clear, and lively sentences are general guidelines to use.

4. Ask:

"What did you do to combine the sentences?"

Writing their responses on the board will help them when they work on their own pieces. Their responses might include: combined two short sentences with *and* or *but,* moved one word or phrase from one sentence to another.

Application
1. Hand out "Techniques Used to Combine Sentences" and compare what is on this list to the one written on the board. This comparison will show the students that they already knew how to combine sentences, but they need to apply their knowledge to their writing.

2. Ask students to read through their rough drafts, highlighting short sentences that can be combined. Then using the handout and the list on the board, combine the sentences in their rough drafts.

3. Circulate about the room, assisting students that need additional instruction. Students finishing their work early can help others.

Assessment
As students finish, ask three or four to write their before sentences and their revised sentence on a transparency to show the class. Seeing the revisions helps the students understand the techniques used to combine sentences.

Minilesson 28

Transparency

SENTENCE COMBINING PRACTICE

DIRECTIONS: Combine the sentences in the paragraph below to make it more clear and concise.

The bell rings to dismiss class. The students pour into the halls. The halls are crowded. Students stop at their lockers for books. Students need books for their next class. Students stop at their lockers to put books away. Students stop to talk to their friends. Students must weave their way through the halls. Clusters of students stop at the water fountains to socialize. Teachers stand in the halls. Teachers try to keep the students moving to their next class. The teachers also watch for students fighting in the halls. Students fighting in the halls rarely happens. The bell rings for class to begin. The principal is Mr. Manning. Mr. Manning escorts the tardy students to class.

Sample Revision:

The bell rings to dismiss class, and students pour into the crowded halls. They stop at their lockers to get books for their next class, to put books away, and to talk to their friends. Students must weave their way through the halls because clusters of students stop at the water fountain to socialize. Teachers, standing in the halls, try to keep the students moving to their next class. Teachers also watch for students fighting in the halls which rarely happens. After the bell rings to begin class, the principal Mr. Manning escorts the tardy students to class.

Minilesson 28
Transparency/Handout

TECHNIQUES USED TO COMBINE SENTENCE

1. Combine sentences using coordinating conjunctions: *For, And, Nor, But, Or, Yet, So*; referred to as FANBOYS.

example: The bell rings to dismiss class. The students pour into the halls.

revision: The bell rings to dismiss class, *and* the students pour into the halls.
(remember the comma)

2. Combine sentences by inserting modifiers, usually adjectives or adverbs.

example: Students pour into the halls. The halls are crowded.

revision: Students pour into the *crowded* halls.

3. Combine sentences using prepositional phrases.

example: Students stop at their lockers to get books. Students need books for their next class.

revision: Students stop at their lockers to get books *for their next class.*

4. Combine sentences by listing items in a series with commas and the conjunction *and.*

example: Students stop at their lockers to get books for their next class.
Students stop at their lockers to put books away.
Students stop to talk to their friends.

revision: Students stop at their lockers to get books for their next class, to put books away, *and* to talk to their friends.

5. Combine sentences by showing their relationship to one another using subordinating conjunctions .

example: The students must weave their way through the halls.
Clusters of students stop to talk to their friends.

revision: Students must weave their way through the halls *because* clusters of students have stopped to talk to their friends.

Minilessons for Revision–©1997 Absey & Co., 23011 Northcrest, Spring, Texas 77389, 281.257.2340

Minilesson 28
Transparency/Handout

TECHNIQUES USED TO COMBINE SENTENCE
CONTINUED

6. **Combine sentences using participle phrases, a phrase beginning with the *-ing,* *-ed, -t, -n,* or *-en* form of a verb and is set off by commas.**

   example: The teachers stand in the halls.
                 The teachers try to keep the students moving to their next class,
   revision: The teachers, *standing in the halls,* try to keep students moving to their next class.

7. **Combine sentences using adjective clauses, a dependent clause beginning with the relative pronouns: *which, that, whom, whose,* or *who.***

   example: The teachers also watch for students fighting in the halls.
                 Students fighting in the halls rarely happens.
   revision: The teachers also watch for students fighting in the halls *which* rarely happens.

8. **Combine sentences using appositives, a phrase that renames or identifies a noun and is generally set off by commas. Essential appositives are usually proper nouns and are not set off by commas, but this is not always the case.**

   example: The principal is Mr. Manning.
                 Mr. Manning escorts tardy students to class.
   revision: Mr. Manning, *the principal,* escorts tardy students to class.

9. **Combine sentences using adverb clauses, a dependent clause beginning with the subordinating conjunctions: *after, although, as, because, before, if, since, than, that, though, unless, until, when, where,* or *while* and set of by commas.**

   example: The bell rings to begin class.
                 The principal Mr. Manning escorts tardy students to class.
   revision: *After the bell rings to begin class,* Mr. Manning, the principal, escorts tardy students to class.

Minilessons for Revision–©1997 Absey & Co., 23011 Northcrest, Spring, Texas 77389, 281.257.2340

Minilesson 29

Skill
Varying Sentence Beginnings

Objective
Students will be able to identify the part of speech or type of phrase/clause their sentences begin with and recognize repetitive beginnings, then vary the sentence beginnings to make their rough drafts more interesting to read.

Materials
Teacher: poster of "Variations of Sentence Beginnings"
Student: rough draft
pen/pencil
highlighter
paper

Procedure
1. Instruct students to highlight the first few words of every sentence.

2. Then, instruct them to fold a piece of paper in half lengthwise and list the first few words of every sentence on one half.

3. Explain to students that visually seeing the first words of their sentences heightens their awareness of the tendency to start each sentence with the same type of beginning, which lowers the impact of their writing.

4. Ask two or three students to read their list of first words, or partial list depending on the length of the list, as you write them on the board.

5. Post "Variations of Sentence Beginnings" and review the parts of speech and types of phrases/clauses listed.

6. Then, identify the part of speech or type of phrase/clause of each word on the board.

7. Next, circle the repetitive words, repetitive types of phrases/clauses, and repetitive parts of speech in each list on the board.

8. Model on the board how to change the repetitive sentence beginnings using "Variations of Sentence Beginnings".

Application
1. Ask students to identify the part of speech of each word or type of phrase/clause they listed in the first column on their paper, then circle the repetitive words, repetitive types of phrases/clauses, and repetitive parts of speech.

2. Students may find this difficult, so be prepared to circulate the room to offer individual help. Students finishing quickly can help those needing additional help.

3. Instruct students to change the words or phrases they circled to vary their sentence beginnings in their rough drafts. As students become proficient with this technique, challenge them to use every beginning on the chart.

Assessment
1. Allow students to work in pairs, comparing their changes and offering suggestions for more and better changes.

NOTE: Sometimes sentence structure becomes awkward and contrived when the revisions are made. Students need to be allowed to make the decision to keep their original sentence. If the desired results aren't achieved using these techniques, suggest to students that combining sentences might achieve better results.

2. Ask students to write their before and after sentences on the board, stating which variation they used. Allow the class to assess the sentences for accuracy and quality.

Idea adapted from *Acts of Teaching*

Minilesson 29

Transparency/Poster

VARIATIONS OF SENTENCE BEGINNINGS

NOUN	Jeff practices basketball four hours a day.
PRONOUN	He plays on varsity, so he has to be good.
ARTICLE	The coach starts him in every game.
INFINITIVE	To win the game is Jeff's ultimate goal.
GERUND	Playing tonight's game is no exception.
ADVERB	Quickly, Jeff flies down the court.
PARTICIPLE PHRASE	Receiving the ball from center, Jeff scores.
ADVERB CLAUSE	While the crowd screams, Jeff catches his breath.
PREPOSITIONAL PHRASE	In the next three minutes, Jeff scores four points.
ADJECTIVE	Purple and white wins again tonight.

Minilessons for Revision—©1997 Absey & Co., 23011 Northcrest, Spring, Texas 77389, 281.257.2340

USE CONCRETE METHODS TO TEACH MECHANICS

Overview and Rationale

The minilessons in this chapter are taught interactively, engaging students physically in the lessons. This helps them learn the rules they must know in order to punctuate their writing correctly. From these lessons, students will learn the critical role punctuation plays in conveying their intended message. Also, by using concrete items to illustrate a concept or by creating a visual image, students will remember the rules and concepts so they can apply them in authentic situations.

"Comma Rules Made Easy" should be one of the first lessons taught as it will be frequently referred to in other lessons. It is important for students to work with these four rules all year so they can apply them correctly and add new rules as they use them.

As grammar should be taught within the context of a students' writing, so should mechanics. Teaching dialog within the framework of a student's narrative makes it especially easy for him or her to learn the many ways of punctuating dialog and the intricate paragraphing needed among different characters. This also helps ensure the transfer of the information from short to long term memory.

Minilesson 30

Skill
Comma Rules Made Easy

Objective
Students will be able to identify four major comma rules, then apply them correctly in their writing.

Materials
Teacher: poster of "Four Ways to Use A Comma"
3 different colors of sentence strips
1 roll of adhesive magnetic strip

Student: rough draft
pen/pencil
highlighter

Getting Started
The minimum time investment spent preparing this lesson will save maximum time grading all year because students will use commas correctly. Prepare the materials once and use them year after year.

Write the following words or parts of a word on one color of sentence strips, cut them to size, and glue magnets on the back of the strips.

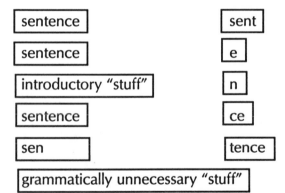

sentence	sent
sentence	e
introductory "stuff"	n
sentence	ce
sen	tence
grammatically unnecessary "stuff"	

Write all of the coordinating conjunctions vertically on one piece of the same color sentence strip.

For
And
Nor
But
Or
Yet
So

Write the following punctuation marks and

words on a 3 x 3 piece of sentence strip in a second color. Glue magnets on the back of the squares.

13 squares with a comma
1 square with a *but*
2 squares with an *and*
8 squares with a period

Write each part of the model sentences below on sentence strips in a third color, cut to size, and glue magnets on the backs of the strips.

the seniors planned a parade for homecoming

the rain prevented it from taking place

after long hours of hard work

the students felt disappointed and frustrated

Jerry

the class president

asked the principal if the parade could be rescheduled

Jerry promised the principal good weather

full student participation

sponsor supervision

Procedure
1. Explain:
"The comma is the punctuation mark that is used most often because it is essential for determining meaning."
2. Brainstorm with the students all the ways they know how to use a comma. (This is a good review.) Then ask:
"Which ones give you the most problem?"
Chances are they will be the four you are going to teach. List them on the board:
• joining two complete sentences with a conjunction
• after introductory "stuff" in a sentence
• setting off unnecessary "stuff" in a sentence
• a series in a sentence
3. Hand out all of the prepared sentence strips, making sure every student has at least one strip. If magnets are not on the back of the strips, have a supply of sticky tack on hand to put up the strips.
4. Start with the first rule and ask two students with the word *sentence* on a strip to put

them on the board. Explain:

"Two relating sentences, or independent clauses, can be combined with a coordinating conjunction and a comma."

Then, ask a student with a comma to put a "," square on the board after the first *sentence*. This is a perfect time to explain a comma splice.

Next, explain coordinating conjunctions using the FANBOYS acronym, and ask the student with the FANBOYS strip to put it on the board. And finally, ask for the end punctuation to be put on the board. Remove all strips from the board.

5. Proceed with the remaining three rules, following the model in step 4. In Rule 2, explain *introductory stuff* can be a phrase beginning with a preposition, a prepositional phrase; a clause beginning with a subordinating conjunction, an adverbial clause; or a phrase beginning with a participle, a participial phrase. In Rule 3, explain *unnecessary stuff* as an appositive, a phrase that renames or identifies a noun. Essential appositives are usually proper nouns and do not need to be set off with commas.

6. When all four rules are posted, begin with Rule 1, and put the model sentences on the board. Ask:

"Who has a sentence that could be an independent clause?"

Put up the sentence. Then ask:

"Who has a sentence that relates to this sentence?"

Put it on the board, leaving space between the two independent clauses. Now ask:

"To join these two independent clauses, what do we need between them?"

If students respond with, "a comma," allow them to put a "," square on the board then explain a comma splice and ask:

"What do we need to correct a comma splice?"

Put the FANBOYS strip on the board. Then ask a student to put the end punctuation on the board.

7. Proceed with the three remaining model sentences, following the model in Step 5.

8. Students have learned interactively four ways to use a comma. Ask for questions and put up the poster. Instruct the students to write the rules and examples in their notebooks.

Application

1. Instruct students to quickly look through their rough drafts to find an example of each rule. Write a student example on the board under the rule to which it applies.

2. Working individually, instruct the students to reenter their rough drafts and highlight the FANBOYS. Then check the words before and after the FANBOYS to determine whether or not a comma needs to be inserted. Remind them that FANBOYS are not always used to join two independent clauses.

3. Instruct students to look at the first words in every sentence to determine whether or not a comma needs to be inserted after *introductory stuff*.

4. Instruct students to look for *unnecessary stuff* after the subject or other nouns of each sentence and insert commas if they are needed. If an appositive is a proper noun, a comma is not usually needed.

5. Instruct students to look for a series of three or more words or phrases that need to be separated by commas and insert them if needed.

6. Instruct students to look at any long sentence, over ten or twelve words, to see if a comma is needed.

Assessment

To reinforce the rules, put students with a partner and instruct them to explain the rule for the comma placement in their piece. Instruct them to delete the comma if there is not a valid rule for its placement. The rule may or may not be one of the four stressed in this lesson.

Adapted by Kay McCormack from *Acts of Teaching* (Carroll 190)

Minilesson 30

Transparency/Poster

FOUR WAYS TO USE A COMMA

1. Insert a comma between two independent clauses (sentences) that are joined with a coordinating conjunction (F-A-N-B-O-Y-S).

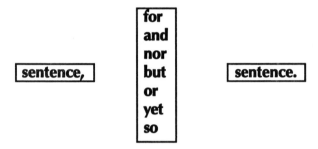

| for |
| and |
| nor |
| but |
| or |
| yet |
| so |

| sentence, | | sentence. |

| The seniors planned a parade for homecoming | , | but | the rain prevented it from taking place. |

2. Use a comma after long *introductory stuff* at the start of a sentence.

| introductory stuff | , | sentence. |

| After long hours of hard work | , | the students felt disappointed and frustrated. |

3. Use two commas to set off grammatically *unnecessary stuff* from the rest of the sentence.

| sen | , | grammatically *unnecessary stuff* | , | tence. |

| Jerry | , | the class president | , | asked the principal if the parade could be rescheduled. |

4. Use a comma after each item in a series.

| sent | e | , | n | , | and | ce. |

(main part with item one) (item two)   (item three) (rest of sentence)

| Jerry promised the principal | good weather | , | full student participation | , | and sponsor supervision | for the parade. |

Minilessons for Revision–©1997 Absey & Co., 23011 Northcrest, Spring, Texas 77389, 281.257.2340

Minilesson 31

Skill
Making Sense with Semicolons
("Commas Made Easy" should be taught before this lesson)

Objective
Students will be able to recognize where to place a semicolon, then reenter their rough drafts to determine if semicolons are needed.

Materials
Teacher: poster of "Three Ways to Use a Semi-
          colon"
          3 different colors of sentence strips
          1 roll of adhesive magnetic strip
Student: rough draft
          pen/pencil
          paper

Getting Started:
The minimum time investment spent preparing this lesson will save maximum time grading all year because students will use commas correctly. Prepare the materials once and use them year after year.

Write the following words or parts of words on one color of sentence strips, cut them to size, and glue magnets on the back of the strips.

sentence		se		c
sentence		n		e
sentence		t		
sentence		e		
conjunctive adverb			n	

Write the following punctuation marks and words on a 3 x 3 piece of sentence strip in the second color. Glue magnets on the backs of the squares.

8 with a semicolon	8 with a comma
6 with a period	2 with an "and"
1 with "however"	

Write each part of the model sentences below on the third color of sentence strip, cut to size, and glue magnets on the backs.

Professional athletes are idolized by society

children look up to them for role models

Sport heroes posses money and honor

they abuse their positions by breaking the law

Some of the fallen heroes are Pete Rose

catcher for the Cincinnati Reds

Mike Tyson

heavy weight boxing champ

Michael Irvin

wide receiver for the Dallas Cowboys

Procedure
1. Explain:
    "A semicolon helps connect two independent clauses and helps prevent confusion in sentences containing commas."

2. Hand out all of the prepared sentence strips, making sure every student receives at least one. If magnets are not on the back of the strips, have a supply of sticky tack on hand to put up the strips.

3. Start with the first rule and ask two students with the word *sentence* on a strip to put them on the board side by side. Explain two relating independent clauses or sentences can be joined with a semicolon instead of a comma and a FANBOYS (refer to "Comma Rules Made Easy"). Ask a student with a ";" to put it on the board between the two sentences. Then ask for the student with the end punctuation to put it on the board after the second sentence.

4. Clear the board and then follow the above procedure, proceeding with the remaining two rules (see p. 71).

5. When the rules are posted, begin with rule one and put the model sentence on the board under the rule. Ask:
    "Who has a sentence that could be an independent clause? Who has the relating independent clause?"
Put them on the board. Then ask:
    "How can you correctly punctuate this sentence using a semicolon?"
Put the semicolon between the two independent clauses and a "." at the end.

6. Proceed with the two remaining model sentences.

7. Instruct students to copy the rules and

examples in their notebooks.

Application

1. Instruct students to work with a partner to write an original sentence for each rule.

2. Ask students to share their sentences. Write at least one sample for each rule on the board.

3. Most students will not have semicolons in their writing. If they do, ask them to check for proper use. If they don't, ask them to read through their rough drafts, looking for at least one place to use a semicolon.

Assessment

Ask students to share a sentence with a semicolon from their revised rough drafts.

Minilesson 31

Transparency/Poster

THREE WAYS TO USE A SEMICOLON

1. **Use a semicolon to connect two independent clauses without a coordinating conjunction (FANBOYS).**

   | sentence | ; | sentence. |

   | Professional athletes are idolized by society | ; | children look to them for role models. |

2. **Use a semicolon to connect independent clauses that are joined by a conjunctive adverb:** *also, consequently, finally, for example, however, instead, later, nevertheless, and therefore.*

   | sentence | ; | conjunctive adverb | , | sentence. |

   | Sport heroes posses money and honor | ; | however | , | they abuse their positions by breaking the law. |

3. **Use a semicolon to separate items in a series if those items have internal commas.**

   | sen | , | t | ; | e | , | n | ; | and | c | , | e. |

   (main part) (item one) (item two) (item three)

   | Some of the fallen heroes are Pete Rose | , | catcher for the Cincinnati Reds | ;

   | Mike Tyson | , | heavy weight boxing champ | ; and | Michael Irvin | ,

   | wide receiver for the Dallas Cowboys | .

Minilessons for Revision–©1997 Absey & Co., 23011 Northcrest, Spring, Texas 77389, 281.257.2340

Minilesson 32

Skill
Punctuating Dialog

Objective
Students will be able to use paragraphs, quotation marks, end marks, and commas correctly in dialog, then reenter their rough drafts to correct punctuation and paragraphing of dialog.

Materials
Teacher: 4 copies of "Sample Passages with Dialog"
characters' name or role written on 5 x 7 card
poster of "Rules for Punctuating Dialog"
Student: rough draft
pen/pencil

Procedure
1. Ask four students to volunteer to read to the class. Instruct the students reading the dialog to stand side by side in front of the room. Give each student a name tag for the character he or she is portraying, and the same passage of dialog. Ask them to read their character's lines, taking a step back each time they read to signify indention, after they read their dialog, students step back up to the line. The fourth person will read the explanatory material, the information not in quotes, standing by the person speaking. This illustrates that explanatory material goes with that character and should be in the same paragraph.

2. When the reading is complete, ask the students why the characters stepped back when they spoke and stepped up when they finished speaking. Point out to students that every time a new person speaks, a new paragraph begins.

3. Ask students:
"What moves when I speak and stops moving when I am silent?"
Answer:
"My lips. Much the same way quotation marks work. They signal that someone is speaking. When and how to use quotation marks is easy to remember if you think of them as two lips (Carroll 189)."

4. Post the "Rules for Punctuating Dialog" on the board and ask students to write them in their notebooks.

Application
Ask the students to check for proper punctuation and paragraphing in the dialog they have written in their piece, using the rules posted.

Assessment
Instruct students to exchange papers with a partner to check their dialog for punctuation and paragraphing.

Minilesson 32

Transparency/Poster

RULES FOR PUNCTUATING DIALOG

1. Each time a new character speaks, a new paragraph should begin.

2. Everything a character says should be in quotation marks.

3. Use a comma to separate an explanatory phrase from the quotation. Place it outside the opening quotation marks, but inside the closing quotation marks.

   example: Jack said, "Jill, let's go up the hill."
   "We need a pail of water," Jack said.

4. Place an exclamation point, question mark, or period inside the closing quotation mark except when questioning or exclaiming about a quote.

   example: "Don't fall down the hill!" Jill exclaimed.
   Jill asked, "Jack, did you break your crown?"
   Jack replied, "Of course not, Silly."

Minilessons for Revision–©1997 Absey & Co., 23011 Northcrest, Spring, Texas 77389, 281.257.2340

Minilesson 32

Transparency/Poster

SAMPLE PASSAGE WITH DIALOG

"Why is this taking so long? She has been in surgery for six hours," Ms. Osborne anxiously asked the nurse.

The nurse looked at her tear-stained face and tried to comfort her. "Dr. Kneely is a thorough surgeon. If he found more damage than the x-rays showed, he will repair it, regardless of the time it takes to do it. Please try to remain calm."

"I can't stay calm! My beautiful daughter is lying in surgery, fighting for her life because of an idiotic drunk driver." Ms. Osborne could barely speak through her tears.

Just then, Mr. Osborne arrived from the airport. He had been in California on a business trip when he received the call about his daughter's wreck. "Melissa, how is Jan? Is she going to be all right?"

"I don't know yet, Gary. She has been in surgery for six hours, and the nurse doesn't know why."

"Melissa, tell me what happened? Why is my baby here?"

"Oh Gary, Jan was crushed by the door. It took the fire department two hours to cut her out of the car. Her spine is broken, and she is bleeding internally. The doctors aren't sure what the extent of her injuries are. There is a strong possibility of paralysis."

"How did it happen?"

Melissa tried to stop the flood of tears as she told her husband the events that led up to the wreck. "Jan went to the mall with Amy. On their way home, a drunk driver ran a red light, plowing into Jan's side of the car. Someone called 911, and I received a call from the hospital that she was here in critical condition. Amy sustained minor injuries, and she is home with her parents. The drunk driver is sitting in jail, and I'll see to it that he rots there."

Chapter 6

PROOFREADING AND EDITING THE FINAL COPY

Overview and Rationale

The skills of editing and proofreading are key to writing as a process. Editing is altering or refining the writing and is usually done by another person. The lesson "Editing for Economy" enables the student to understand that quality writing is tight and concise. Proofreading is reading for detail and making corrections on a final copy and is usually done by the writer. Both skills are combined in the proofreading lessons in this chapter.

Students benefit from these proofreading and editing lessons because they hear an explanation of each skill for which they proofread or edit, then immediately apply it for a genuine reason. Immediate application of a skill taught and reinforced within a student's writing furthers the probability of retention and transfer of information.

Higher grades is another benefit students receive from proofreading and editing. They find the "stupid mistakes" such as misplaced commas, misspelled words, words written twice, and words omitted; then they have the opportunity to correct these mistakes before their writing is evaluated. A bonus for the teacher is grading papers with fewer mistakes, making the task easier and more enjoyable.

Minilesson 33

Skill
Editing for Economy

Objective
Students will be able to identify words and phrases that are unnecessary for meaning, then reenter their rough drafts and edit for economy.

Materials
Teacher: transparency of "Sample Passage to Model Editing"

transparency of "Techniques Used for Editing"

Student: rough draft

pen/pencil

highlighter

Procedure
1. Explain:

"Good writing is tight; every word and phrase carries meaning, verbs are powerful, and nouns are specific. To achieve the goal of concise, tight writing is difficult because the writer has to step away from the writing, look at it objectively, and be willing to eliminate the unnecessary words."

2. Put "Sample Passage to Model Editing" on the overhead and read it with the students. They will agree that the passage is quality writing and needs no revision.

3. Put "Techniques Used to Edit" on the overhead and instruct students to copy them in their notebooks. This transparency could also be used for a poster.

4. Put "Sample Passage to Model Editing" back on the overhead and ask students to look at each word or phrase that could be eliminated without changing the meaning, using "Techniques Used to Edit." Put brackets around the words and phrases they suggest. A transparency with suggested changes has been included.

5. Read the passage without the bracketed words and ask the students which passage they prefer and why.

Application
1. Ask students to read their rough drafts and try to eliminate twenty words. The number will vary depending on the length of the rough drafts and the proficiency of the students. Start with a low number and make it higher every time students edit a paper.

2. Ask students to find a partner and read the sentences that contain bracketed words. Do they both agree that the words can be eliminated without changing the meaning?

Assessment
Ask students to share sentences containing words they eliminated.

Minilesson 33

Transparency

SAMPLE PASSAGE TO MODEL EDITING

The media and the entertainment world propagate America's fascination with alien life forms and unidentified flying objects. Movies such as *Independence Day* and television series such as *Third Rock from the Sun* and *Star Trek* spark the interest of even the most dull imaginations. Cartoon and comic book super heroes invade the daydreams of children. Best-selling science fiction authors Arthur C. Clark and Robert Silverberg keep readers frantically turning the pages of their books, clamoring for more. People know these stories and characters are fantasy, but when they read news headlines and hear special reports about UFO sightings, the general populous begins to seriously question the possibilities.

It is the speculation about the existence of planets and life forms beyond our solar system that gives astronomers and scientists the incentive to search the galaxies. Scientists have developed equipment to monitor radiation activity in outer space, and NASA has satellite stations in space in hope that other planets can be discovered. Astronomers search the skies with high-powered telescopes, looking for unknown planets orbiting around unknown stars. The discovery of other solar systems by scientists or astronomers will radically change the world in incomprehensible ways.

The quest to discover what lies beyond our solar system will not cease until scientists and astronomers can answer the question, "Does life exist on other planets?" Until then, Americans can ponder the probability that aliens exist and enjoy the entertainment about other worlds and their inhabitants.

Minilessons forRevision–©1997 Absey & Co., 23011 Northcrest, Spring, Texas 77389, 281.257.2340

Minilesson 33

Transparency of Suggested Changes

SAMPLE PASSAGE TO MODEL EDITING

The media and [the] entertainment world propagate America's fascination with alien life forms and unidentified flying objects. Movies such as *Independence Day* and television series such as *Third Rock from the Sun* and *Star Trek* spark the interest of [even] the [most dull] dullest imaginations. Cartoon and comic book super heroes invade [the] children's daydreams [of children]. Best-selling science fiction authors Arthur C. Clark and Robert Silverberg keep readers frantically turning the pages [of their books], clamoring for more. People know these stories and characters are fantasy, but when they read news headlines and hear special reports about UFO sightings, the general populous begins to [seriously] question the possibilities.

[It is the] speculation about the existence of planets and life forms beyond our solar system [that] gives astronomers and scientists the incentive to search the galaxies. Scientists have developed equipment to monitor radiation activity in outer space, and NASA has satellite stations in space [in hope that] hoping other planets can be discovered. Astronomers search the skies with high-powered telescopes, looking for unknown planets orbiting around unknown stars. The discovery of other solar systems [by scientists or astronomers] will radically change the world in incomprehensible ways.

The quest to discover what lies beyond our solar system will not cease until scientists and astronomers can answer the question, "Does life exist on other planets?" Until then, Americans can ponder the probability [that aliens exist] of alien existence and enjoy the entertainment about other worlds and their inhabitants.

Minilesson 33

Transparency

TECHNIQUES USED FOR EDITING

- **Eliminate unnecessary prepositional phrases.**

  example: members [of the group]   group members

- **Eliminate modifiers that mean the same as the word they modify.**

  example: smiled [happily]   [quickly] ran

- **Eliminate sentences repeating the same information or almost the same information.**

- **Eliminate adjectives that describe the obvious.**
  example: [big] ocean   [loud] crash

- **Eliminate the unnecessary *that, which*, and *who*.**

  example: I knew [that] he left.
             Empty the pitcher [that] contains the tea.
  revision: Empty the pitcher containing the tea.

- **Eliminate the unnecessary *the*.**
  example: Alex assumes [the] responsibility for his actions.
             [The] students left the gym.

Minilessons forRevision–©1997 Absey & Co., 23011 Northcrest, Spring, Texas 77389, 281.257.2340

Minilesson 34

Skill
Proofreading in Small Groups

Objective
Students will be able to identify errors in the writing of their classmates, then reenter their writing to make the necessary corrections.

Materials
Teacher: 2 or 3 blank transparencies for each student
1 non-permanent transparency pen for each student (4 different colors of pens)
paper clips
correction fluid
Student: final copy of their piece

Procedure
1. Explain:
"Proofreading is an important step in the writing process. We all make minor errors when we write because it is difficult for us to be objective. Also, when we proofread and edit our own papers, our eyes see what our brain thinks; we know what we meant to write. Therefore, we need objective eyes to proofread and edit our papers, and those objective eyes can be a classmate, another writer, or trusted reader."

2. Handout paper clips and 1 blank transparency for each page of the student's final copy. Instruct students to paper clip a transparency to each page of their final copy, including their cover sheet.

3. Explain:
"The purpose of this activity is to find errors in spelling, grammar, and mechanics, not problems with organization. It is too late in the process for major problems to be revised. It is not up to the proofreader to correct the paper, but it is his or her responsibility to catch the mistakes and mark them. If a proofreader is not sure about a mistake, mark it anyway. It is better to find each other's mistakes before the teacher or evaluator does."

4. Divide students into groups of four or five, and give each student in the group a different color of transparency pen.

NOTE: When the authors get their papers back with corrections, and they have a question about one, they will know whom to ask if each person in the group has a different color pen.

5. Instruct students to pass their final copy, with a transparency paper clipped to each page, to the person on their right.

6. Then, ask students to check the cover sheet for the following items:
   • first and last name
   • date
   • class period
   • title, no quotation marks, and not underlined

If students find a mistake or an item missing, they mark it on the transparency.

NOTE: This step will lower the teacher's frustration level when grading the papers because the information on the cover sheet will be correct.

7. Then, instruct students to pass the papers to the right again and ask them to check the paper for commas. Write *COMMAS* and the editing marks used for commas on the board. It is a good idea to review the four comma rules and put up the poster for students to refer to while they are checking the paper. If the students find an error in the paper, instruct them to mark the mistake with the appropriate editing mark on the transparency.

8. When all of the papers have been checked for commas, instruct students to pass the papers to the right again. Now, ask students to check the paper for spelling and double or omitted words, write *SPELLING* and the editing mark used for spelling on the board. Instruct students to start at the end of the paper and look at it from right to left. They will be able to focus on the individual words if they are not reading the paper. Students mark the misspelled words with the editing mark.

NOTE: If the majority of your students are using spell check on a word processor, instruct them to check for the use of *to, too, two*; *there, their, they're*; *its, it's*; *your, you're*; or other homophones.

9. Repeat this process until the students have proofread and edited the papers for the remaining details to be checked. Proofread and edit for the skills taught in minilessons during the writing of the paper and skills taught in minilessons for previous writing assignments.

Application

1. When the authors' papers are returned to them, they need to determine whether or not the mistakes marked are valid by using a dictionary, referring to their notes or a grammar handbook for specific rules, discussing the mistake marked with the editor/proofreader who marked it, or checking with the teacher. If a mistake is valid, the author *must* correct it in class using correction fluid. This is important because if students copy their papers over, they make new mistakes.

    NOTE: Be aware that students using word processors will want to make the corrections on the computer before turning their paper in.

2. Circulate about the room answering questions for the students.

3. Instruct students to clean off the transparencies when they have completed correcting the mistakes found in their papers. Keep a supply of inexpensive diaper wipes for this purpose.

Assessment

1. After the corrections are made, instruct students to staple their cover sheets and final copies together, then turn them in.

2. When the students turn in their papers, place a check by their names on a class roster or in the grade book. Immediately, the teacher will know who did not turn in a paper, and in the event a student says, "I turned it in," the teacher will have a way to verify whether or not he or she did.

Minilesson 35

Skill
Proofreading with Group Experts

Objective
Students will be able to recognize mistakes in grammar, mechanics, and spelling in the writing of their classmates, then reenter their final copy to make necessary corrections.

Materials
Teacher: small sticky notes, 4 - 6 per student
white correction fluid
grammar handbooks
dictionaries
Student: final copy
pen/pencil

Procedure
1. Explain:
"Proofreading/editing is an important step in the writing process. We all make minor errors when we write because it is difficult for us to be objective about what we have written. Also, when we proofread/edit our own papers, our eyes see what our brain thinks; we know what we meant to write. Therefore, we need objective eyes to proofread/edit our papers. Each of you will choose to be an expert in the field of writing based on your strengths. You may think you don't have a strength, and if you don't, choose a field you enjoy because you will become an expert." Explain the following:

Mechanics Engineer: This person is an expert in maintaining the meaning of sentences through the correct use of punctuation marks: commas, semicolons, quotation marks, and end marks.
Their function in the group is to examine every paper for correct use of punctuation, and their main tool is a grammar handbook.

Word Specialist: This person is an expert in recognizing misspelled words and the incorrect use of homophones: *to, too, two; their, there, they're; it's, its;* and others. Their function in the group is to examine every paper for words with questionable spelling and the correct use of homophones. Their main tool is a dictionary.

Master Grammarian: This person is an expert in detecting incorrect use of the English language: subject/verb agreement, pronoun antecedents,

and complete sentences. Their function in the group is to examine every paper for problems in usage, and their tool is a grammar handbook.

Master Proofreader: This person is an expert in reading for meaning. Their function in the group is to check for proper sequence of events, organization, maintaining reader's interest, clarity of writing, and cohesiveness of the writing. Their tool is a sharp mind and the ability to recognize quality writing.
NOTE: The teacher needs to know how many groups there will be so he or she will know how many students are needed in each field. Each group needs one person from each field. Write the four fields and the number of students needed in each field on the board. As students choose an expert field, write their name under the field they chose. Then, divide the students into groups of four, placing one student from each field in every group. Sometimes it will be necessary for the teacher to serve as one of the group members to make the groups even.
2. Give each expert his or her tool, a dictionary or grammar handbook, and each student several sticky notes.
3. Each student proofreads/edits all four papers in his or her group for the area of expertise he or she chose. When an error is found, instruct the students to place a sticky note on the paper, then write the error on the sticky note. Students should not write on another student's paper.

Application
1. After the experts have proofread/edited the papers in their group and returned them to the authors, the authors must determine whether or not the noted error is valid. They do this by checking the rules in a grammar handbook, looking up words in the dictionary, discussing the error with the expert, or asking the teacher. If the error is valid, students will want to correct their mistakes in class with correction fluid. If they copy their paper over, they make new mistakes.
NOTE: Be aware that students using word processors will want to make the corrections on the computer before turning their paper in.

2. Circulate about the room, answering questions for the students.

Assessment

1. After the corrections are made, instruct students to staple their cover sheets and final copies together, then turn them in.

2. When the students turn in their papers, place a check by their names on a class roster or in the grade book. Immediately, the teacher will know who did not turn in a paper, and in the event a student says, "I turned it in," the teacher will have a way to verify whether or not he or she did.

Chapter 7

IDEAS FOR EVALUATION

Overview and Rationale

The suggestions and minilessons in this chapter deal with ways to evaluate writing by the teacher, by peers, and by the writer. The minilessons teach writing skills that students have applied to their pieces during the revision process. Students have worked diligently to improve their writing by revising their writing and making decisions on their own and with the help of their peers. For this reason, it is important that students' writing be evaluated by more than one person.

Because evaluating writing is subjective, it is often difficult to determine a grade. However, this is not the case when students are involved in determining the criteria for evaluation. Involving students in this process allows them to feel the grade they receive is fair and justifiable. By giving the students a portion of the responsibility for evaluation, teachers have more justification in making the final determination of a grade.

Evaluating writing that has been extensively revised for specific skills requires a different approach, and the advantages of changing the evaluation process are significant. Since the students' revisions have been evaluated during the process, it is not always necessary to evaluate the revisions made on the rough drafts at the time the final copies are evaluated. By not requiring students to turn in their rough drafts and prewriting with the final copies, the overwhelming paper load is lessened. Also, a paper that has been revised and proofread by students before the final evaluation by the teacher has fewer mistakes and is better quality. This makes the evaluation of the final copy a more enjoyable and less time-consuming experience.

A Helpful Hint

Before returning the students' papers, choose three papers to use as models to explain the differences between an *A*, a *B*, and a *C*. Without telling the students the grade, read one of the papers, and ask the students, "Would this paper be an *A*, a *B*, or a *C*?" Students will choose the grade the paper received because they know what quality writing is intuitively . Then, read another paper and ask the students, "Would this paper be an *A*, a *B*, or a *C*?" Read the last paper even though they know what grade it received.

Then make three columns on the board and at the top of each column write one letter grade. Starting with the *A* paper, discuss the qualities each paper possess. Ask students, "What does the *A* paper have that the *B* paper doesn't? What does the *B* paper have that the *C* paper doesn't." Write their responses on the board under the appropriate column. The students should notice the following:

use of figurative language
clearly organized
choice of vocabulary
lack of boring descriptions
lead hooks the reader
interesting content
powerful verbs
clearly written

When the discussion is complete, return the students' papers. They will immediately understand why they received their grade, and they will know what they can do on the next paper to improve their grade.

Another Helpful Hint

When grading a paper, make no comments on the paper, instead, record notations in pencil on the grading scale. On the student's paper, place a small check in the margin on any line that has a mistake. If there are two mistakes in one line, make two checks in the margin. Then, when you return the papers to the students, ask them to correct the mistakes in their papers using a different color of ink. This makes it easier for you to find their corrections.

By giving students the opportunity to correct the mistakes they make in their writing, they will learn why they made the mistakes and hopefully not make them again. This also reinforces the skills the students must know in order to write well.

After students have corrected the mistakes, re-evaluate the papers for the corrections. These can be used as daily grades.

Minilesson 36

Skill
Developing a Grading Scale
(This should be done 3 or 4 days prior to the due date of the final copy.)

Objective Students will be able to develop a grading scale based on the concepts taught during the process of writing their piece.

Materials
Teacher: a list of skills taught during the writing of the piece

Procedure
1. Explain:
"A grading scale is used to evaluate writing so students know exactly what the basis is for the grade."

Brainstorm a list of skills that should be evaluated. The skills taught during the process of writing the paper should be included as well as the skills students should already know. For example:

> *Skills Taught*
> > commas
> > lead
> > using imagery
> > *be* verbs
> > content
> > pronoun antecedents
>
> *Previous Skills*
> > events in proper sequence
> > basic paragraph structure
> > capitalization rules
> > spelling
> > end punctuation
> > complete sentences

2. Write the list on the board, then ask students to group similar items together. For example:

> **I.** spelling, commas, capitalization, end punctuation
> **II.** paragraphs, sequence
> **III.** *be* verbs, pronoun antecedents, complete sentences
> **IV.** imagery
> **V.** content, lead

3. Next, ask students to suggest a heading for each group. Invariably they will suggest:

> **I.** mechanics,
> **II.** organization,
> **III.** grammar,

> **IV.** style,
> **V.** content.

4. Once the headings are established, determine what percent of 100% each section should be. Explain to the students that the skills taught during the process should carry more weight than the previously learned skills. With teacher guidance, the students will generally come to the same conclusion as the teacher. For example:

content	50%
mechanics	15%
organization	15%
grammar	15%
style	<u>5%</u>
	100%

5. When the grading scale has been finalized, ask the students to write it down so they will know how their papers are to be evaluated.

NOTE: The "Sample Grading Scale" will give some ideas about format.

Application
Students will apply this skill when they do the lesson "Peer Evaluation."

Assessment
Students can be assessed for their participation in the process of developing a grading scale.

Minilesson 36

Transparency

SAMPLE GRADING SCALE

Name_____ Title _____

I. MECHANICS - 15 Possible Points					Points Earned _____	
Correct Use of Punctuation	4	6	8	9	10	_____
Spelling and Capitalization	1	2	3	4	5	_____

COMMENTS _____

II. ORGANIZATION - 15 Possible Points					Points Earned _____	
Logical Sequence	4	6	8	9	10	_____
Paragraph Structure	1	2	3	4	5	_____

COMMENTS _____

III. GRAMMAR - 15 Possible Points					Points Earned _____	
Use of *be* Verbs	1	2	3	4	5	_____
Pronoun Antecedent	1	2	3	4	5	_____
Complete Sentences	1	2	3	4	5	_____

COMMENTS _____

IV. STYLE - 10 Possible Points					Points Earned _____	
Use of Imagery	1	2	3	4	5	_____

COMMENTS _____

V. CONTENT - 50 Possible Points					Points Earned _____	
Lead (specific, grabs attention)	4	6	8	9	10	_____
Topic Covered	4	6	8	9	10	_____
Reader Appeal and Attention	4	6	8	9	10	_____
Clear Focus	4	6	8	9	10	_____
Evokes Emotion	4	6	8	9	10	_____

COMMENTS_____

_____

_____

_____ + _____ + _____ + _____ + _____ = _____
I.   II.   III.   IV.   V.   Grade

Minilessons for Revision–©1997 Absey & Co., 23011 Northcrest, Spring, Texas 77389, 281.257.2340

Minilesson 37

Skill
Peer Evaluation

Objective
Students will be able to recognize specific details in the final copy of their paper, then evaluate the final copy for the correct application of those specific details.

Materials
Teacher: copies of grading scale for every student (see "Developing a Grading Scale")

Student: final copy
pen/pencil

Procedure
1. Explain:

"The purpose of peer evaluation is twofold. Students learn to see writing as a reader and learn how to objectively evaluate writing for quality. Also, evaluation is a skill used on most tests. When a writer can evaluate someone else's writing, his or her own writing will improve."

2. Before students turn in their papers, hand out the grading scales and ask them to fill in the top two lines. Students should turn in a grading scale paper clipped to their final copy.

3. After students have turned their papers in, give each student who has turned in his or her paper someone else's final copy, making sure no one is given his or her own paper.

NOTE: It is also successful to have students evaluate papers from another class.

4. Instruct the student evaluators to put their ID # at the bottom of the grading scale. This gives the evaluator more freedom to be honest.

NOTE: In order for the evaluators to be held accountable for their evaluation, the teacher must know who the evaluator is.

5. Instruct students to read the final copy through one time before they make any comments on the grading scale.

6. On the second reading, instruct students to look for the items listed on the grading scale. Remind them NOT to make any marks on the paper. All comments and questions should be written on the grading scale.

7. Explain:

"Comments need to be made in each section of the grading scale and the comments should be specific. For example:

"Don't write, 'Your description is good'; write, 'Your description of the dog is good because I could see the color, feel the soft fur, and hear his loud bark.'"

Application
Instruct students to evaluate the papers, writing their comments on the grading scale.

Assessment
1. When students finish the evaluation, pick up the final copy with the grading scale. This evaluation will not be handed back to the author until the paper has been evaluated by the teacher. If the evaluations are handed back to the authors at this point, the students feel the need to question their evaluator. This can cause mayhem in the room and does not allow the evaluators freedom to be honest in their evaluation.

2. Since the main function of this lesson is the evaluation process, a grade could be given to the evaluator for his or her evaluation.

Minilesson 38

Skill
Self-Evaluation of Writing

Objective
Students will evaluate their own writing in order to determine what they have learned and how they have learned it, the strengths and weaknesses of their writing, and improvements they can make for quality writing.

Materials
Teacher: copies of "Self-Evaluation Form" for every student
Student: final copy
pen/pencil

Procedures:
Explain:
"The purpose of evaluating your own writing is to help you recognize the strengths and weaknesses in your writing, and determine what you can do to improve on the weaknesses and build on the strengths. Knowing how to evaluate will help you when you take tests. Self-evaluation will also help you make the connection between the effort you put forth and the grade you receive. But most importantly, by stating what you have learned and how you have learned it, you will begin to recognize your learning style."

Application
1. Hand out a self-evaluation form to the students. Instruct them to read their piece, then thoughtfully and honestly answer the questions.
2. When they have completed the form, it should be turned in with their final copy.

Assessment
As students become accustomed to self-evaluation, it will become easier for them to evaluate themselves. Self-evaluation will help them become aware of how they learn and what they can do to improve their learning process

Minilesson 38

Transparency/Handout

SAMPLE OF SELF-EVALUATION FORM

Name _____   Title _____

Answer the following questions thoughtfully and honestly.

What is the strength of this piece? _____
_____

Why? _____
_____
_____
_____

What are the weaknesses of this piece? _____
_____

How could I improve the weaknesses in this piece? _____
_____

What did I learn from writing this piece? _____
_____

How did I learn it? _____
_____

On a scale of 1 to 5, with 5 being the highest, how much effort did I put forth to write this piece? _____

What grade do I deserve on this piece? _____ Why? _____
_____
_____
_____

AFTERWORD

The task of writing this book has been more grueling than I had anticipated, but served as a learning experience I would not have missed. The purpose of the book is to share with teachers the lessons that have helped my students and me become better–they at writing, me at teaching. It is the culmination of how I have taught writing, and what I have learned from students about their processes of writing.

It is my hope that this book will benefit teachers who want to teach writing as a process and desire to move away from the traditional methods of teaching writing to a more meaningful and effective approach. These lessons can help teachers understand the nature of writing and demonstrate a way to teach that encourages students to write.

Teaching writing as a process means trying new ideas and altering lessons previously taught in order to motivate students to achieve quality writing. It means questioning the assignments and the methods used to teach those assignments in order to determine if they are valid. Teachers should ask themselves if their lessons are incorporating brain based learning, multiple intelligences, and learning styles. This approach means taking risks that sometimes fail, but more often succeed.

Teachers who embrace the philosophy of writing as a process will discover, much like I did, their teaching methods revolutionized, and their students enthused about writing. Teaching will once again be exciting and enjoyable because the students will claim ownership of their writing, take responsibility for their efforts, and produce quality writing.

When students become independent writers, they become independent learners–equipped for life.

Works Cited

Atwell, Nanci. 1987. *In the Middle: Writing, Reading, and Learning with Adolescents*. Portsmouth, NH: Boyton/Cook and Heinemann Educational Books.

Brandvik, Mary Lou. 1990. *Writing Process Activities Kit*. West Nyack, NY: The Center for Applied Research.

Calkins, Lucy McCormick. 1994. *The Art of Teaching Writing*. Portsmouth, NH: Heinemann Publishers.

Carroll, Joyce Armstrong and Edward E. Wilson. 1993. *Acts of Teaching: How to Teach Writing*. Englewood, CO: Teacher Ideas Press.

Gwodz, Jon. 1994. *Timeless Treasures*. Crowley, TX: Crowley Ninth Grade Campus.

Huff, Chris. 1995. *Dreamscapes*. Crowley, TX: Crowley Ninth Grade Campus.

Lane, Barry. 1993. *After the End: Teaching and Learning Creative Revision*. Portsmouth, NH: Heinemann Publishers.

Llano, Lisa. 1994. *Timeless Treasures*. Crowley, Tx: Crowley Ninth Grade Campus.

Marsden, David. 1994. *Timeless Treasures*. Crowley, TX: Crowley Ninth Grade Campus.

Miller, Marcy. 1995. *Dreamscapes*. Crowley, TX: Crowley Ninth Grade Campus.
Murdock, Justen. 1995. *Dreamscapes*. Crowley, TX: Crowley Ninth Grade Campus.

Muschla, Gary. 1993. *Writing Workshop Survival Guide*. West Nyack, NY: The Center for Applied Research.

Neeld, Elizabeth Cowan and Kate Kieefer. 1990. *Writing: Brief Third Edition*. Glenview, IL: Scott, Foresman/Little, Brown Higher Education.

Pearce, Brian. 1994. *Timeless Treasures*. Crowley, TX: Crowley Ninth Grade Campus.

Richardson, Kenji. 1995. *Timeless Treasures*. Crowley, TX: Crowley Ninth Grade Campus.

Rief, Linda. 1992. *Seeking Diversity: Language Arts with Adolescents*. Portsmouth, NH: Heinemann Publishers.

Sebranek, Patrick, Verne Meyer, and Dave Kemper. 1992. *Write Source 2000*. Burlington, WI: Write Source Educational Publishing House.

Sousa, David A., 1995. *How the Brain Learns*. Reston, VA: The National Association of Secondary School Principals.

Vygotsky, L. S. 1978. *Mind in Society*. Cambridge: Harvard University Press.

Weaver, Constance. 1996. *Teaching Grammar in Context*. Portsmouth, NH: Boynton/Cook Publishers, Inc.

Index